JEWS IN CONTEMPORARY EAST GERMANY

Jews in Contemporary East Germany

The Children of Moses in The Land of Marx

Robin Ostow

St. Martin's Press   New York

First published in the United States of America in 1989

Printed in Hong Kong

ISBN 0-312-03118-1

Library of Congress Cataloging-in-Publication Data
Ostow, Robin.
  Jews in contemporary East Germany : the
children of Moses in the land of Marx/Robin Ostow.
  p.   cm.
  Includes transcriptions of twelve taped interviews,
nine being translations from the German.
  Bibliography: p.
  Includes index.
  ISBN 0–312–03118–1
  1. Jews—Germany (East)—History.   2. Holocaust survivors
—Germany (East)—History.   3. Germany (East)—Ethnic relations.
I. Title.
DS135.G332085   1989
943.1′004924—dc19   89–30606
                                                              CIP

This book is dedicated to
Natascha, Naomi and Nurit

Contents

Part III Two Interviews Conducted in West Berlin

Acknowledgements

It goes without saying that this kind of project could be carried out only with strong support on both sides of the 'Iron Curtain'. My work benefited immensely from the advice, help, and encouragement of many people and institutions on two continents, although I assume final responsibility for the text.

The first thanks go to those most directly involved; the interviewees, the Internationales Pressezentrum, and the Jewish Community in East Berlin for their gracious cooperation. The transcription, translation and editing of the twelve tapes and the research for the first and last chapters were generously supported by a grant from the Social Sciences and Humanities Research Council of Canada. The American Jewish Committee, the American Joint Distribution Committee, and the Leo Baeck Institute in New York, and the Library of the Jewish Community in West Berlin all offered me access to their documentary resources, and their staff members provided much-appreciated advice and help. Thomas Sandberg of East Berlin provided several of the photos.

In Berlin, West Germany, and Switzerland, ideas and encouragement in various forms came from David Bathrick, Claus Offe, Friedemann Büttner, Hajo Funke, Jochen Blaschke, Franz and Verena von Hammerstein, Aron Bodenheimer, Monika Richarz, Annegret Ehmann, Klaus Scheurenberg, Tom Strauss, and Eva Kaminer. Thanks also to Julius Schoeps and the Salomon Ludwig Steinheim Institute for German Jewish History.

In Toronto Gregory Baum, Robert Brym, Gerry Gold, Frances Henry, Klaus Hermann, Iwona Irwin Zarecka, Margie Wolfe, Gail Bennick and Meyer Symiotyckie provided support and suggestions, especially in the later phases of developing the raw interviews and data into a book. Cordula Hacke and Edith Dierker transcribed the tapes, Shirley Fulford typed the final text, William Cunningham provided technical assistance, and Campus Reproductions handled the photocopying.

In the USA many thanks are due to Frank Mecklenburg, Michael Riff and Marion Kaplan at the Leo Baeck Institute, Gene Du Bow at the American Jewish Committee, and Denise Gluck at the American Joint Distribution Committee; also to Kurt Wolff, George Ross, Gerson Cohen, Eli Ginzberg, Gerry Bubis, Phyllis Freeman, Shari Friedman, and to my parents Miriam and Mortimer Ostow.

I also wish to thank my editors, Simon Winder and Susan Kemp at Macmillan, and Annalisa Vivieni at Jüdische Verlag bei Athenäum, for the energy, skill and care with which they turned my manuscript into a book.

Michael Bodemann is responsible for the fact that I ever got to East Berlin. He read and commented on every chapter, supplied photos for the book, and put up with endless discussions of what Jewish life in the GDR is (and is not) all about.

My children Natascha, Naomi, and Nurit graciously accommodated themselves to my work schedule and itinerary. They are the reason for undertaking this kind of project in the first place.

Finally, there are three people without whom this enterprise would have been impossible. They prefer to remain anonymous, but they know who they are, what they have accomplished, and how much it is appreciated.

Robin Ostow
Berlin

1 Introduction
Survival and Metamorphosis: The History of the Jewish Community of East Berlin

In the first third of this century Berlin was a world centre of Jewish life, and the site of many of the most important developments in Jewish thought and practice. In 1925 its Jewish population of 172 672[1] was served by more than a hundred synagogues, twelve of which contained over 2000 seats.[2] It was in Berlin that Reform Judaism germinated and evolved its early institutions. In 1904 the Jewish Feminist Movement was founded in Berlin and, in 1928, for the first time in Jewish history, a woman delivered a sermon from the pulpit of a major Reform synagogue in Berlin. When Hitler came to power in 1933, Berlin's Jewish population had already declined to 160 564; and by the time of the first deportations from Berlin in autumn 1941, the Jewish population was estimated at 65 000. When the Allies liberated Berlin three and a half years later, in the first week of May 1945, they found slightly more than 7000 Jews still alive in the city.

The story of how a handful of Jewish men around Martin Riesenburger kept themselves alive, buried the dead according to Jewish tradition, and maintained some Jewish observances in the Weissensee Cemetery – even through the darkest days of 1944 and early 1945 – is narrated movingly in Riesenburger's book *Das Licht verlöschte nicht* (1960/1984). At risk to their own lives, these men hid 560 Torahs in the cemetery, thus saving them from the Nazis and from the destruction of the Allied air raids, and they contributed to the morale of many Jews who were in hiding or living under false identities, by distributing illegal copies of the Jewish calendar and conducting illegal prayer services. On Friday, 11 May 1945, three days after the liberation of Berlin, Martin Riesenburger officiated at public Friday evening services at the Weissensee cemetery chapel, and at the end of July 1945, he again presided over a Bar-Mitzva and a Jewish wedding in Berlin.

For the Jewish Community of Berlin – which was officially reconstituted on 15 July 1945 – the first years after the war were characterized by instability and in-fighting among both the leadership and the grass roots, as the small group of survivors struggled to develop working relationships with all four occupying forces and to weld its own culturally balkanized membership into a unified polity. The first President, Erich Nelhans, a former Mizrachi leader, was arrested by the Soviets in 1947 and charged with aiding Soviet military deserters. He was sentenced to 15 years imprisonment, and has not been heard from since.[3] In fall 1945 Nelhans was succeeded by Hans Erich Fabian, a lawyer and the only member of the old *Reichsvereinigung* to survive the war. In 1949 Fabian emigrated to New York where he worked for many years on the negotiations for restitution payments to Jewish survivors of Nazism.

Also in autumn 1945, the American Joint Distribution Committee (also referred to as the AJDC or 'Joint') began to actively support the Berlin Jewish Community which then numbered 7070 members. Of these 7070 Jews, 4121 (over 90% of all married members) had non-Jewish spouses, 1321 had come out of hiding, and 1628 had returned from concentration camps.[4] And in other respects as well, the *Jüdische Gemeinde* of the early post-war days bore little resemblance to our current North American and West European stereotype of a fairly homogeneous community of affluent professionals, business people, scholars and artists. Philip Skorneck, one of the first AJDC representatives in Berlin, made the following observations – among others – in his first reports filed 21 February 1946 and 31 March 1946.

> I arrived in Berlin on October 15.
> The *Jüdische Gemeinde* had reorganized itself immediately after the liberation of Berlin and had established offices and shelters in various houses which had previously been the property of the organized Jewish Community...an 'election' had been held in the *Jüdische Gemeinde* two weeks before I reached Berlin. It subsequently appeared that this was an election in name only.
> Unfortunately, there was considerable question about the personal honesty of [the Jewish leaders] and I have since come to believe that this question had some basis in fact. Mr. Meyer,[5] for instance returned from the concentration camp without a mark and is now a very wealthy man.
> The Jewish community itself is a complex and confusing one. There are full Jews, half Jews and quarter Jews and there are Jewish Protestants, Jewish Catholics and there are Jews married to non-Jews without children and there are Jews married to non-Jews with children who are either Jewish or non-Jewish and each of these categories had a different status under Hitler.
> Inherent in the high incidence of what might be called 'marginal Jewishness' among the Berlin population is the problem of determining which 'Jews' should be permitted to qualify for membership in the *Gemeinde*.
> As it began to appear that accredited Jews in Berlin might receive certain advantages and privileges over the general population:

particularly when the Joint began to distribute supplementary food to the members of the *Gemeinde*, loud protests began to be heard from those who were considered ineligible for membership.

Strains and tensions between the Polish and German Jews [have] been apparent in Berlin. The Polish Jews, recently arrived from Poland, are wont to make constant remarks regarding the questionable Jewish character of the *Gemeinde* members and the *Gemeinde* members in turn do not miss an opportunity to remark on the high degree of black marketing practice among the Polish Jews.[6]

That Jewish life became disorganized and that individual Jews became demoralized and brutalized by their experience of Hitler's Final Solution is not to be wondered. And in the early post-war years life in Berlin generally was a chaos of individuals and interest groups seeking to establish – or re-establish – themselves and competing for limited material and social resources. Particularly impressive was the speed with which Jewish life was re-established in the city as a result of the combined efforts of the AJDC, the occupying powers, and the Berlin Jewish Community. Jewish residents, refugees and Displaced Persons were clothed, fed, housed and given medical attention. Thousands of Jewish survivors who passed through Berlin were sent on to Israel, the Americas, and other areas as well. Synagogues and other Jewish institutions were re-opened, and a campaign was initiated to demand the return of confiscated Jewish property and the recognition of the Jewish Community by the governing institutions.

By 1949 the leadership of the Berlin Jewish Community had stabilized around Heinz Galinski (b. 1912) who still leads the Jewish Community of West Berlin today. The first five years of Galinski's term of office involved, among other challenges, the problems of maintaining infrastructure and social and religious services in all four zones of the divided city in the face of the mounting pressures of the Cold War.

> The Community tried to preserve a neutral attitude and maintain the community as a non-political organization above and beyond any party struggle. For a number of years the Berlin organization provided the only instance of an organizational setup which included both East and West Berlin. The religious and social needs were dealt with by a board comprised of five representatives from the West and two representatives from the Eastern sector.[7]

As the Cold War set in, however, it became more and more difficult to operate in both sectors of the city and, by late 1952, it became impossible. 'The...year 1952 had seen a "consolidation" of the DDR...by which was meant an increased rate of Sovietization in all fields of public life' (Robinson, 1954, p. 85).

The anti-Jewish line started in the DDR in mid-December 1952, when the Central Committee of the SED [Socialist Unity Party] issued a 60-page circular dealing with the lessons of the Slansky trial. The circular pointed out the importance of Zionism and international Jewish organizations, such as 'Joint', as 'agencies of American imperialism', which misused the sympathy of working peoples for Jewish victims of fascist persecution in order to organize espionage and sabotage in the peoples' democracies.

(Thompson, 1967, p.63)

This circular was followed by accusations against Jews in the Party press, the purging of many Jews from positions of power, and increased supervision of Jews in the GDR. The leaders of the East German Jewish Communities were interrogated and asked to sign statements which denounced the AJDC as an organization of American agents, equated Zionism with Fascism, protested the death sentence passed on the Rosenbergs, and condemned the campaign for restitution payments as exploitation of the German people.

Nathan Peter Levinson who was then Rabbi in Berlin[8] described the reactions within the Berlin Jewish Community as follows;

> This was the big fight with Galinski. He was not happy that...after the Slansky trials...Seeing the new anti-Semitism...I called a press conference to ask the Jews to leave [the GDR]. And Galinski refused to attend this press conference: tried to prevent me from giving it, because he felt I was pursuing an American policy and not a Jewish policy.
>
> 'Til the last minute they tried to prevent me...they threatened me...but I felt it was necessary to do what I did because we had one Holocaust and if Stalin hadn't died miraculously...
>
> One day after I called the press conference Galinski also called for the Jews to leave – I forced his hand – but internally he blamed me.
>
> Before we did this, we moved most of the Jewish library which was in East Berlin over to West Berlin. We didn't want to leave anything which was important.
>
> (Taped interview, Toronto, November 1984)

Meanwhile, many Jews in the GDR and the leaders of all its Jewish Communities had, on their own, decided to flee to the West. The first group of 25 arrived in West Berlin on 13 January 1953. Over the winter the anti-Jewish measures were stepped up. The homes of almost all Jews were raided, identity cards were seized, and victims were ordered to stay close to home. The largely Jewish VVN (Union of those persecuted by the Nazis) was dissolved and replaced by the Committee of Anti-Fascist

Resistance Fighters which had a much less Jewish character, and the purges of Jews from prominent positions were continued and extended to even those Jews who supported the government's anti-Zionist, anti-American and anti-restitution positions. By 30 March 1953, approximately 550 Jews had fled the German Democratic Republic; and Stalin's death on 5 March heightened the uncertainty and tension among Jews in all sectors of the divided city.

Some of the effects of these events on Jewish communal life in West Berlin are described in a report from the AJDC Paris office dated 6 March 1953, *Newsletter on Jewish Life in Berlin*:

> Although being in the minority, the National Jewish faction [of the West Berlin Jewish Community] has by its step of founding the Zionist Organization taken the initiative in a pronounced more 'Jewish' course and thereby also inadvertently given a clear answer to recent developments in the East...
>
> While it is the aim of both factions of the *Gemeinde* to preserve the unity, the National-Jewish faction is not willing to make concessions on 'Jewishness' or to disclaim orthodox or national-Jewish aspirations...Rabbi Levinsohn (Liberal) takes an uncompromising stand against national and orthodox aspirations and on several occasions has publicly denounced Zionism in his sermons.
>
> Thus the *Gemeinde* holds on to the ideal of unity in the face of mounting difficulties.
>
> All difficulties...outlined in foregoing paragraphs are of recent origin and clearly in connection with the new anti-semitic tendencies in the East... Thus the larger conflict of two opposing worlds also draws into its orbit the small Jewish Community of Berlin.
>
> (AJDC Paris letter No. 130, stencilled)

By mid-June 1953 the stream of Jewish refugees from the GDR to West Berlin abated, and within the GDR there was an abrupt change of policy; the measures against Jews ceased and the rehabilitation of the Jews and their Communities began. The small remnants of the Jewish Communities in the GDR became the recipients of large government grants to repair and renovate synagogues (Thompson, 1967, p. 97), to maintain the Jewish Home for the Elderly, the kosher butcher, and the Jewish cemeteries in East Berlin; they also publish a quarterly Bulletin, the *Nachrichtenblatt*. Jews now living in the German Democratic Republic receive special pensions as Victims of Nazism and partial pensions for any physical damage suffered under Hitler. The GDR Constitution grants complete freedom of faith to all its citizens: it allows religious associations to regulate and administer their own affairs; and guarantees the right to give religious education (*Christians and Churches*, 1983, p. 70). Thus since 1953, the GDR government has been more than cooperative in all matters regarding Jews, as will become clear in the interviews.

In Berlin, once the Jewish Community had split and the West Berlin Community had set up new headquarters in the Joachimsthalerstrasse, a provisional executive committee was constituted in the East to condemn the leaders who had fled and to deal with the state authorities. Martin Riesenburger, who had publicly supported the GDR government during the crisis, became Rabbi of East Berlin.[9] He has since become known as the 'Red Rabbi'; although he was considered a mere apologist for his government by many West German Jews, he was a very loved and honoured figure in East Berlin where he served as the only Jewish religious functionary until his death in 1965.

Heinz Schenk became President of the Jewish Community of East Berlin; he held this position as a paid officer of the state, and served until his death in 1971. Schenk had been a member of the SED since 1945, and has been accused of imposing the Party's will on the Jewish Community (Lesser, 1973, p. 15, n. 2). At Schenk's death, the post of President of the Jewish Community became an elective and an honourary one. Dr Peter Kirchner (see Chapter 2) was elected to succeed Schenk. Dr Kirchner still administers the *Jüdische Gemeinde* with a Board of Directors composed of five members elected by and from the general membership of the East Berlin Jewish Community.

In spring and summer 1956 many Jewish government officials and artists who had been purged in the early 1950s were rehabilitated, and today Jews are once again found in visible and influential positions in the German Democratic Republic: most of the Jews in this category, however, are not members of the Jewish Community, but Communists who settled in the Soviet occupied zone. Richarz (1985) emphasizes that 'most of these Communists staunchly refused to consider themselves Jews, and none became a member of the Jewish communities. Membership in the atheist Communist Party was not compatible with religious identity which additionally would have increased the danger of being accused of Zionist tendencies' (p. 127). One of the most powerful Jews in the GDR is Albert Norden who is a member of the Politburo, the group of ten men who lead the SED. Klaus Gysi, the Minister for Church–State Affairs from 1979 to 1988, is of partly Jewish descent, and Gerhard Eisler, also a Jew, served for many years as head of the GDR Office of Information.

Thus, at the official level, far from being a persecuted minority, since 1953, Jews in the GDR have become a 'protected species': according to the GDR government pamphlet *Christians and Churches: A Report from the German Democratic Republic* (1983),

> Fascism and racism have been extinguished and banned in the GDR, and along with them, every form of anti-Semitism. Jewish citizens have complete rights and liberties to practice their religion...

Every year, on 9 November, the people of the GDR recall the horrors of the Nazi Pogrom during the *Kristallnacht*, the night in 1938 when the Nazis began their open slaughter of the Jewish population. And each September, when the Victims of Fascism are remembered, wreaths are laid in Jewish cemeteries. (p. 54–5).

Some of the implications, subtleties, and omissions of these statements, as well as the more concrete experiences of living as a Jew in the GDR today will be explored in the interviews which follow. The interviews also contain basic information on the demography, finances, activities of the East Berlin Jewish Community, which have not been elaborated here to avoid repetition and to give the Jews of East Berlin – in so far as possible – the chance to tell their own story.

My own interest in Jews and Jewish life in East Berlin was awakened long before I had any idea that the story was so dramatic. From September 1982 to September 1984 I was living with my husband and our three children in West Berlin. A Jew moving to the former Nazi capital obviously has more than the usual culture shock to deal with in the process of settling in; and during my own sojourn the confrontations – difficult under any circumstances – were heightened by the aftermath of the Israeli invasion of Lebanon in June 1982 and the angry reactions in many West European capitals. Moreover in West Germany – and particularly in West Berlin – the year 1983 marked the fiftieth anniversary of Hitler's rise to power. The occasion was observed through a series of public ceremonies, exhibits, publications and performances. That winter the occurrences in the Middle East combined with the commemorative events in the Federal Republic gave rise to a renewed and intensified soul searching among Germans and Jews alike.

As I was struggling to come to terms with the complex and burdened reality of Jewish life in West Berlin, a Jewish acquaintance in East Berlin invited us, in March 1983, to the Purim celebration at the synagogue on the Rykestrasse in East Berlin. The experiences and friendships that resulted directly and indirectly from this visit – and the implicit contrasts and continuities with Jewish life in West Berlin – raised a series of questions about Jewishness and Judaism, and their place in European – and particularly in post-war German – society and their role in a socialist society. The four specific issues which informed the selection of interviewees and the questions asked were:

(a) In the North American Jewish tradition, socialism is associated with a secular interpretation of Jewishness. In East Berlin, however, Judaism is defined as a 'faith' and Jewishness is transmitted and acquired through – by North American standards – very orthodox and restrictive criteria. The seemingly harmonious combination of political socialism and religious traditionalism challenged my previous assumptions and called for clarification.

(b) I was interested in the relationship of the East German Jewish Community to the state and to the Socialist Unity Party. Especially against the background of the liberalization of the East German State's relationship with its churches, I wanted to learn more about the role of Jews and the Jewish Communities in public life, and the reconciliation of the apparent contradiction between the internationalist – one could even say 'melting pot' – idealogy of the Communist Party and the particularism inherent in any specifically Jewish organization.

(c) On a more concrete level I hoped to explore the continuities and contrasts with Jewish life in West Berlin in terms of both the individual and the Jewish Community: this includes the degree and parameters of communication between the two Jewish Communities and areas of cooperation, competition, and conflict.

(d) My final concern was the effect of being Jewish on the work experience, personal life, and world view of individual Jewish citizens of the German Democratic Republic.

Preliminary archival work confirmed that few of the above issues had been seriously examined. Many articles have been published about Jews in the GDR, but most represent crude Communist or anti-Communist propaganda. Statistics and lists of religious objects locally available (and unavailable) substitute for the study of social processes; thoughtful analysis is sorely lacking.

In the interviews and concluding essay which follow, the basic statistical and infrastructural data about the Jewish Community in East Berlin is provided as a point of orientation, but the emphasis is rather on the qualitative aspects and the dynamics of Jewish life in East Berlin at the level of the individual and of the Jewish Community. Finally, this should be seen as a preliminary rather than a definitive exploration of problems which, through the peculiarities of recent German history, have become far more important and complex than the small number of Jews still living in the German Democratic Republic would suggest.

The ultimate credibility and value of a series of interviews conducted across the 'Iron Curtain' rests, to some extent, on the richness of detail and the relevance and inner logic of the discussions with the individual interviewees. These qualities can be judged by each reader. But even this evaluation can take place only in the context of an understanding of how the twelve interviewees were selected and the conditions under which the interviews were taped. Names of possible interviewees were selected with the idea of including representatives of both genders and of several age groups. The voices of members of the organized Jewish Community were to be heard, as well as the views of those who chose not to join:

and the sample was to include members and non-members of the SED. Finally, individuals were sought who might not only articulate a personal style and *weltanschauung*, but who could explore the structure of the Jewish Community and its role in East German society from the point of view of a particular relevant office or academic discipline. Two dimensions that might have been considered but were not – largely due to lack of time – are Jewish life outside East Berlin and Jewish life in different social classes in the GDR.

With input from knowledgeable friends, a preliminary list of approximately eighteen names was compiled and submitted to the International Press Centre in East Berlin for approval. Three people who have a great deal to contribute to the discussion of Jewish life in the GDR but who refused to be interviewed are Klaus Gysi, then GDR Minister for Church –State Affairs, and Professors Marie and Heinrich Simon of Humboldt University. It is hoped that at some point their experiences and insights will become accessible to the public in some form. One individual on the list consented to be interviewed, but was denied permission by the authorities. Other names were crossed off the list because people were out of town at the time the interviewing was to take place and/or seemed less important on second consideration, and one or another name was added. In the end, eleven people were interviewed over the summer of 1984. These eleven include the first ten interviews in the text and one interview which is not published. The eleventh interviewee refused to let me tape our discussion, which left me legally vulnerable. Moreover the reporting of his remarks and behaviour would not have contributed much to the exploration of Jewish life in the GDR.

The first ten interviews in the text were taped in East Berlin. The inteviews with Irene Runge and with Alfred and Ursula Katzenstein were conducted in English: their words are their own. The other seven interviews were taped in German and later translated into English. In the GDR an interview is not a private event between two people and a tape recorder. It is more like a marriage in that it is mediated by the state, and a representative of the state is present. Thus the eleven interviews taped in the GDR were administered through the offices of the International Press Centre. They took place at the Press Centre and at the homes and offices of the interviewees, and they were supervised by an IPC staff member.

The two final interviews were taped in the fall of 1983, in West Berlin, in German and were later translated into English. The circumstances of the taping of the interview with Helmut Eschwege are explained immediately before the text of that interview. History does not stop between the taping of an interview and its publication. Rather than change the text, or introduce more footnotes, when appropriate, the interviews are updated in a short paragraph at the end of the text. Updates are as of autumn 1987.

I
The Jewish Community Seen
from Within

Peter Kirchner

2 The Jewish Community in East Berlin*

Dr Peter Kirchner

Dr Peter Kirchner has been a member of Berlin's Jewish Community since his birth there in the *Jüdische Krankenhaus* (Jewish Hospital) in 1935. He earned his Doctor of Medicine at Humboldt University in 1959, and he is currently a practicing neurologist specializing in spinal problems. Dr Kirchner has served as President of the Jewish Community in East Berlin since 1971. He is also an editor of *Nachrichtenblatt*, the bulletin published quarterly by the League of Jewish Communities of the German Democratic Republic.

R.O. Were both of your parents Jewish?

P.K. No, my mother was Jewish, my father was a Christian: but he wasn't a religious Christian, and when I was born – it was 1935, just before the enactment of the Nuremberg Laws – my parents decided to have me circumcised and registered with the *Jüdische Gemeinde*. This proved a rather inauspicious decision because I then became a *Geltungsjude* which meant I had to wear a yellow star, and when the *Jüdische Gemeinde* and the Jewish schools were closed, I wasn't allowed to go to school.

On the 27 and 28 of February 1943 the Nazis mounted their so-called *Fabrikaktion* (Operation Factory) in which 12 000 Berlin Jews were rounded up at their work places and brought to the former Jewish old age home on the Grosse Hamburgerstrasse (right near here, by the old Jewish cemetery where Moses Mendelssohn is buried) to be shipped off to concentration camps. My mother and I were among those taken to the deportation centre. But it turned out that such a large number of prisoners could not be processed at once: they just couldn't fit that many people on the train. So they let the *Mischlinge* (those born of mixed marriages) go. I was only half Jewish, albeit a *Sternträger* (one who had to wear the yellow star), and I was released. My father's employer had a Jewish sister-in-law who had emigrated to America, and he knew that my father was married to a Jewish woman. After his shop in Berlin had been bombed out he had re-opened in a small town outside the city, and he told my father: 'Bring the boy with you to us, and somehow we'll

*This interview was originally published in *The Jewish Spectator*, Spring 1987.

take care of him.' So, from early 1943 to May 1945 I was with my father in Neustadt. We lived there as people who had been bombed out in Berlin and therefore had no documents. No one bothered about us until the Red Army came. They checked through the files in the town hall and realized that there was someone in the family who wasn't registered anywhere, but by that time it was much too late for that information to be of any help to the Nazis. Thus we survived, but it was always through accidents.

My mother had been a clerk in a Jewish jewellery store, but in 1938, after *Kristallnacht*, the owner emigrated and she had to do forced labour that was assigned through the Jewish employment office. So she remained in Berlin, and worked in a tailor's shop in the neighbourhood. In this way, by splitting up the family, we all survived the Nazi regime and the war.

R.O.　What kind of work did your father do?

P.K.　My father was a lathe operator: he made typewriter cylinders.

P.K.　And was he in danger too during that time?

R.O.　No. He was a legal Aryan, so he was even entitled to ration cards.

R.O.　What did you do when you were living in Neustadt? Did you go to school?

P.K.　No, I couldn't go to school, but I passed the time somehow. My mother did what she could to teach me something. I memorized some poetry and I did some arithmetic. And when we returned to Berlin in '45, it turned out that as a result of the impact of the war, and especially of the bombing, the other children didn't get so much schooling either, so when I re-registered in school, I ended up in a class that was appropriate to my age.

R.O.　And had your mother been a member of the Jewish Community this whole time?

P.K.　Yes, she was a member, and so was I.

R.O.　Even though she was married to a non-Jew?

P.K.　Right. My father never joined the *Jüdische Gemeinde* because he never converted to Judaism. But my parents were married in 1934, and the law forbidding marriages between Jews and non-Jews didn't come into effect until September 1935. The Berlin *Gemeinde* was always a Liberal community. There were a large number of mixed marriages among its members, and the non-Jewish partner was not always required to convert. My parents had a civil marriage, though: not a Jewish ceremony.

R.O.　Is your wife Jewish?

P.K. Yes. She's also from a mixed marriage, and she's also Jewish through her mother. She was born after the Nuremberg Laws, though, so her parents were no longer allowed to marry each other. For this reason her parents didn't marry until after the war, and she's still classified as being born out of wedlock. As far as I'm concerned, though, it's a Jewish family.

R.O. What was the Berlin *Jüdische Gemeinde* like in the early years after the war, and how did you experience the split in 1953?

P.K. Well, the *Jüdische Gemeinde* reconstituted itself in August 1945, but at that time we hadn't yet returned to Berlin. The first President was Hans-Erich Fabian, a lawyer, who then emigrated to America and lived in New York. He administered the *Gemeinde* from 1947 to '49 from these rooms here (in the Oranienburgerstrasse). In 1949 Galinski became President, and by that time the *Gemeinde* operated out of several offices in both parts of the city, but the administration was here.

The President of the *Jüdische Gemeinde* has always been elected. And at that time there were several groupings within the *Gemeinde*. There was one group around Julius Meyer and Fritz Katten: Katten was then the Chief of Police. This group had a strong Left orientation. Then there was a faction with a Liberal orientation around Galinski. At that time I was still quite young and I didn't follow those things closely. I can only say that of the Meyer–Katten group, no one is left. Katten emigrated to America, and Meyer went to South America. They were politically probably pretty close to a Communist position, but that tendency disappeared completely. What remained was Galinski's crowd and then a second group around Fritz Croner which later moved to the West.

R.O. You describe Galinski's orientation as 'Liberal': what exactly do you mean by that?

P.K. For them it meant a religious interpretation: they didn't want the *Gemeinde* to become very orthodox. Meyer and Katten were both *Cohanim* and both very religious. The earlier leadership of the Berlin *Gemeinde* had always been associated with a very Liberal approach to the religion – something like Conservative Judaism in America – which for Meyer and Katten wasn't good enough.

R.O. So these people were politically Communists and religiously Orthodox?

P.K. Yes. In retrospect it's difficult to understand what was going on in their heads. In those days the Jewish Community was supported by contributions from the American Joint Distribution Committee which sent food and clothing for members of the *Gemeinde*: the food was distributed at the offices on the Joachimsthalerstrasse and the clothing at the synagogue on the Fränkelufer. In 1949 the GDR was founded: at that time Galinski already had an anti-communist orientation, and in January 1953, after several confrontations with other factions, he moved the entire administration of the *Jüdische Gemeinde* to the western part of the city, so that here we had to organize our own administration. And this rejection of the East has characterized Galinski's political line for the entire thirty years that he's held office.

R.O. How would you characterize the Jews who remained with the Jewish Community in the eastern sector?

P.K. It was mainly a question of residence. Some Jews moved to the western part of the city at that time to become eligible for reparation payments, but many were already living – and in fact had always lived – in the area which now belongs to the democratic sector of the city. And from the very beginning in 1945 prayer services have been held here regularly: in those days they were led by Rabbi Riesenburger who worked largely in this area.

R.O. What about the secular Jews? Did they at some point leave the *Gemeinde*?

P.K. We never had a group of secular Jews in the *Jüdische Gemeinde*, though I know such a thing exists, for example, in Yugoslavia where there's an atheist section within the Jewish Community which comprises about 20% of the total membership. And in Poland there is one congregation for those who consider themselves religious Jews, and right next door is the Jewish Cultural Federation which houses the Jewish theatre and the Jewish newspaper. But in Berlin it was always the Jews who had a religious commitment who felt bound to the *Jüdische Gemeinde*. The non-religious Jews never tried to join.

R.O. How many Jews are there altogether in East Berlin?

P.K. Today we can only estimate the total number of Jews from other information. We now have approximately 3900 persons who are recognized as having been persecuted by the Nazi regime, but the *Jüdische Gemeinde* has only about 200 members. So that really only a small part of those who once considered themselves Jewish has maintained any contact with the religion.

R.O. You were active in the Jewish Community's Youth Group in the 1950s. Can you explain a little about what the Youth Group was like then?

P.K. The Youth Group was already located in West Berlin at that time. The nucleus was a group of young people who as children had taken religious instruction together and later continued to meet on Wednesday evenings in the Joachimsthalerstrasse. We used to have a big Chanuka Ball every year at the Potsdamer Platz, right on the border, and people used to come from both sectors of the city. We also went on excursions together and organized a theatre. Cantor Hecht, the Cantor here at the Rykestrasse, was the leader: he then emigrated to America in '53 when the Jewish Community fell apart.

R.O. Did you really have a Jewish theatre here?

P.K. It was an amateur theatre run entirely by the young people. Mostly we performed little plays for the *Gemeinde* at the holidays. For example, we did a cycle of pieces about the Jewish festivals. The shows were staged with very modest means to entertain the members a bit. At that time the *Gemeinde* was still relatively large. We had about 5000 members, of whom 1000 lived in this part of the city and 4000 in West Berlin.

R.O. Did you have a Bar-Mitzva?

P.K. Yes, in 1948 in the synagogue on the Rykestrasse. Rabbi Riesenburger and Cantor Hecht officiated, and I took lessons from Rabbi Levinson who's now in Heidelberg. We were a group of seven boys with a very similar course of development . We were all born into mixed marriages, but most of us had a Jewish mother, and therefore became *Sternträger*. We were all called up to the Torah one after the other to be received into the community of adults. In those days it was a bit difficult to celebrate: we didn't have the kind of big affairs that you have in the West with several hundred guests. With us it was a very small event – more than modest – within the family.

R.O. How long have you been President of the *Jüdische Gemeinde*?

P.K. Since the death of my predecessor in June '71. At first they asked me to take over *ad interim* so that the *Gemeinde* could continue to function. While I was a medical student I had, at Rabbi Riesenburger's suggestion, become *Mohel* for the *Gemeinde*, and in that way I became involved with the administration. Later I was officially elected President.

R.O. How many circumcisions do you do per year?

P.K. The number of circumcisions of newborns is very limited. I circumcise mostly somewhat older individuals, that is, cases where the parents think for a couple of years about whether they want to have the child circumcised. I also circumcise some adults. I usually do between two and four a year. I also do the circumcisions for the other Jewish Communities in the GDR: this year I've already done a couple for the Communities in Dresden and Leipzig.

R.O. In the thirteen years that you've presided over the *Jüdische Gemeinde* what changes have taken place?

P.K.　There are two opposing tendencies developing simultaneously. The first is that when I took over the *Gemeinde* in 1971, we had about 450 members. We're now reduced to about 200 members, and since we're an over-aged population, the number of new members we take in every year can in no way keep up with the number of deaths.

On the other hand, my predecessors always saw to it that prayer services were held regularly on Friday nights, Saturday mornings, and holidays, but they were not very interested in developing an area which I consider very important, namely Jewish culture. I have initiated regular cultural events one Sunday afternoon a month from October to May. We sponsor lectures on historical or literary themes, we have authors come and read from their books, and concerts of religious and folk music. The second thing that I consider very important and that I'm happy about is that I've established a library here with a collection of books on Jewish history and culture. It's true that most of the people who use the library are not members of our *Gemeinde*, but now at least those who are interested in Judaism have the chance to learn something about it, which wasn't the case before. These are the things that I'm proud of, and to that you can add the fact that we have any activity going on here at all.

The number of members who attend prayer services regularly is naturally very small, but we do our best to get a *minyan* together every week. You also have to understand that when fifteen or twenty people come to services here, that's 10% of our membership, which isn't bad compared to other Jewish Communities. I just came back from Florence, and I have to tell you I was quite surprised when I went to synagogue there last Friday night and saw eight people there out of a congregation of 1800. A much higher proportion of our membership attends services regularly.

R.O.　What would you have liked to see happen in the *Jüdische Gemeinde* that you haven't yet been able to effect?

P.K.　Well, what remains problematic is the extent to which we can involve younger people in the activities of the *Gemeinde*. We're continually working to stabilize a group for our young people that would stimulate them to meet regularly and to carry on the tradition. It's very difficult. For one thing, the young people don't come up with many ideas of their own: their interest in these things is more limited than ours was. The times are also different: when we were that age we stuck together to be with others who had experienced what we had lived through in such a strange environment. Our young people are much better integrated into the larger society, so they have less interest in Judaism. Also our work with young people involves none of the Zionist themes that are so prominent in the youth groups of Jewish Communities in the West. Our young people are not possessed with the idea of going to live in Israel.

Rather, they participate in our prayer services, they come to our cultural events, and we're working now to give them a little bit of a push by putting them in contact with other Jewish Communities. We're trying to reactivate the closer ties we used to have with the Jewish Community in Prague: we also have contact with the Jewish Communities in Hungary and Rumania. Over the coming vacation my son is going to Bucharest, Klutsch, and Budapest to see whether he can organize something with the Jewish Youth Groups there.

R.O.　Does the *Jüdische Gemeinde* maintain any relationship with the state of Israel or with any groups within Israel?

P.K.　We correspond with Jews who come from Berlin and who have been living in Israel – in some cases for over forty years. These people are, for the most part, quite old now and are interested primarily in the graves of family members. Also some members of our *Gemeinde* have close relatives in Israel whom they can visit when they've reached retirement, and some people make use of this privilege and go to Israel every year. But we have no contact with any official institutions in Israel. The relationships which the *Jüdische Gemeinde* here maintains with institutions outside the GDR are on a higher level. We have observer status in the European branch of the World Jewish Congress. In Florence I attended a meeting of the International Council for Christians and Jews. I've also participated in conferences of the World Union for Progressive Judaism, and likewise, we've had contact with, from our point of view, the more Liberal Jewish groups, largely in England, but also in America and the Netherlands, but much less with institutions and organizations in Israel.

R.O.　Do you have any contact with the Communist Party in Israel?

P.K.　I personally met Wolf Ehrlich once: he's a German Jew and a member of Israel's Communist Party, and I was also once introduced to the President of the Israeli Communist Party, Meir Wilner, when he visited the GDR as a guest of the Party here. But those were just incidental events: there's no real relationship between the Jewish Communities here and Israel's Communist Party.

R.O.　Are you a member of the Communist Party?

P.K.　I'm not a member of any political party.

R.O.　Have you ever been to Israel?

P.K.　No, not yet.

R.O.　Does the *Jüdische Gemeinde* take a position on developments within Israel?

P.K.　No. We have an agreement with our state institutions that we take no position on the situation in the Middle East, and that no statements about the Middle East conflict are expected of us, because – and that's the positive thing about it – the state does not want to put the Jewish Community in a situation of conflict. We have always emphasized that, after the war, and especially after the mass murder of Jews in Europe, we consider the existence of such a state important and fully justified. But we take a very, very distanced and critical stance toward the political development of the country, and many of their policies – for example, the Lebanon campaign – we just can't approve of. The state knows, however, that it would serve no purpose for the Jewish Communities here to issue a judgement on the war in Lebanon, and that it would only put the people here in a situation of conflict: and, for that reason, this theme has become a bit of a taboo.

R.O.   Given that the *Jüdische Gemeinde* is so over-aged, what are your expectations and hopes for the future?

P.K.   When I took this job thirteen years ago, things seemed much rosier than they do now, and I used to be more optimistic about what I could accomplish through my own involvement. I have to acknowledge that, because of the age structure of our *Gemeinde* and the limited number of new members we take in, in the coming years our membership will decrease, so that in a few years we will probably be down to about 100 members. I'm hoping that our numbers will then stabilize and perhaps increase. But we suffer – as do other organizations – from the fact that these days couples have only one child, and we have no large families. Perhaps we can grow only through larger birth cohorts.

Historically the Berlin Jewish Community maintained its size and stability through immigration. Berlin Jews were always Jews who came to Berlin from the provinces of Prussia, from the area that is now Poland, like Posen, Silesia, etc. and settled here. Many were actually headed for the New World, but they stopped here and stayed. Since the war, we don't have that kind of immigration any more. We have a few Jews who've come to the GDR from the Soviet Union and Poland because they married GDR citizens: but they are very few and we don't expect any significant immigration from those areas. People who leave Hungary or Poland these days go to the West and not to the GDR. In our *Gemeinde* we now have 80 people who are under 60 years old – some are children; in fact, one was just born, a girl though, so no circumcision. A few years down the road, then, we're looking at a membership of about 100.

R.O.   Is there a tendency here, as there is in the West, for children and grandchildren of secular Jews to return to the religion?

P.K.   Our Youth Group has a few people whose parents and grandparents were Jewish but not in any way religious or *Gemeinde* members. These young people are looking for their roots – there was talk of 'roots' at the congress I just attended – and some of them are among the people I've circumcised recently, but the numbers are relatively small.

R.O. What's the size of your administrative staff?

P.K. Our Board of Directors has five people elected from within the *Gemeinde* and another two successors, or deputies, but these are all honorary positions. We also have an administrator who is not a member of the *Gemeinde*, and my wife runs the library. There are 40 employees (non-Jewish) working for the cemeteries, the old age home, and the kosher butcher shop.

R.O. How often does the Board of Directors meet, and what's on the agenda?

P.K. The President and Vice-President meet every week, and the Board meets every six or seven weeks. Most of our planning is administrative: it involves the repair and restoration of important objects, preparations for the holidays and for our cultural programme, arranging Bar-Mitzvas, etc. There are also reports on conferences that we participate in and work on the *Nachrichtenblatt* (Bulletin). Another important area is our social work. All of our members are recognized by the state as Victims of Fascism, and for that they get a good pension – 1350 marks per month: but we take care of any members who have social problems, and we make sure that someone visits our older people, brings them flowers on their birthday, and keeps track of how they're doing.

R.O. Any new projects coming up?

P.K. We're currently putting a new wall up around the Weissensee cemetery. It's just about finished. It cost $2\frac{1}{2}$ million marks, and it's being paid for by the *Magistrat* (Magistrate of the City of Berlin [East]). Next we're putting a new wall around the cemetery of the former ultra-Orthodox congregation *Adas Jisroel* in the Wittlicherstrasse: that should be this year or next year. And then, starting in '86, we want to restore the ruin next door to us – the former synagogue on the Oranienburgerstrasse – which we hope to use ultimately as a museum. That will naturally be a very long-term and expensive project, and it will also be financed by the city.

R.O. What's happened to the extensive properties in this sector of Berlin that used to belong to the Jewish Community?

P.K. The *Jüdische Gemeinde* currently administers only those properties which it can in some way use – that is, this space in the Oranienburgerstrasse, the synagogue on the Rykestrasse, the former orphanage which now houses the old age home, and the cemeteries. The other buildings of the Jewish Community are administered by the state. We agreed to this because there was no way in which we could maintain all those properties. Buildings like the Jewish schools on the Grosse Hamburgerstrasse and the Auguststrasse, the *Rabbinerseminar* (Rabbinical Seminary) and the *Hochschule für Wissenschaft des Judentums* (Institute for the Study of Judaism) are today administered and used by the state. The agreement is that in return the *Jüdische Gemeinde* receives a yearly stipend which enables us to carry out our programme. I get 170 000 marks per year to pay our employees, and an additional 150 000 marks, not in cash, but in labour power that's deployed in our cemeteries. The state also subsidizes our restoration projects. The reconstruction of the synagogue on the Rykestrasse five years ago cost them 600 000 marks.

R.O. Do you see any possibility for more contact between the *Jüdische Gemeinde* here and progressive Jewish groups in the West, and, if so, what form could they take?

P.K. The difficulty is that the initiative would have to come from those who would be interested in working with us. We have contact with the American Jewish Committee. They visited Berlin last year and were received by the State Secretary for Church–State Relations, Mr Klaus Gysi. They've offered us some help: for example they sent us kosher wine for *Pesach* (Passover), and we just received a package from them with *talesim* (prayer shawls), *mezuzot* (doorpost markers), and prayer books. They will also pay a Rabbi to come here from America this year to lead our High Holiday services.

In contrast to the Jewish Communities in other Peoples' Democracies, we don't need the support of the American Joint Distribution Committee which sends, for example, 6000 free meals per day to the Jews in Romania and 10 000 to Hungary. Our people aren't poor, and we don't have those kinds of needs.

AUTUMN 1987

Since 1984 Dr Kirchner – and other functionaries of the Jewish Community as well – have visited Israel where they have represented the Jewish Communities of the GDR at conferences of international Jewish organizations. And plans are now being made for a conference to take place in autumn 1988 in Israel on the theme 'Relations between Israel and the GDR'.

The government of the German Democratic Republic has also announced that over the next six years it will spend 45 million (East

German) marks to restore the remains of the synagogue on the Oranienburgerstrasse for use as a Jewish cultural centre. The building will house a Jewish museum, the Jewish library, and a small sanctuary. It will also contain several conference rooms and a research institute to be dedicated to the study of Jewish regional history.

Sonja Berne

3 Social Work and the Jewish Community in East Berlin

Sonja Berne

Sonja Berne was born in Berlin in 1934. She has been a member of the Jewish Community in Berlin for most of her life and she is currently in charge of the (East Berlin) Jewish Community's programme of social services. In spring 1988, she was elected to the Board of Directors.

S.B. My parents are both living. My mother is Polish, my father, German. My mother is Jewish, my father, Christian. My husband comes from a similar background: we have a Jewish marriage and three Jewish children.

R.O. What was it like to be a Jewish child here in the late 1930s?

S.B. Just terrible! I had Jewish school mates who were then picked up one day in 1942. I saw with my own eyes how they were thrown on a truck together with their parents. It made a lasting impression and I'll never forget it. We were protected because my father refused to divorce my mother. Then in 1942 my mother had me baptized. It was done by a Pastor, not in the church, but in a small room. I can still remember it. At that time I wore my hair piled high on my head, and the way the water rolled over it and then down my face could hardly be described as pleasant. Then, for me, everything was taken care of. Nevertheless, in school they still called me '*die Jüdsche*' (the Jewish one), and the teacher really harassed me.

Once, after I had missed ten weeks of school because I had a severe case of diphtheria and scarlet fever, the teacher dragged me to the front of the classroom, up on the podium from which the teachers used to speak down to the children in those days, and said: 'Look at the Jewish brat: pretty brown eyes but dumb as they come!' I had eight mistakes in my dictation and she used that as an excuse.

R.O. What kind of work did your father do?

S.B. He's a butcher by trade, but then he was drafted into the army. As was usual in the case of mixed marriages, they offered him a car and a piece of land: in fact they offered to make him quite comfortable if he would divorce his Jewish wife. And many non-Jewish spouses did that, but, thank God, I had a father with character who didn't do it. Because of that my father came under the jurisdiction of the OT (Todt Organization) and was sent to do forced labour in a quarry. Many people didn't last very long there, but my father had luck and survived. Then, towards the end of the war, my father came home on leave and decided not to go back. So at the end he was a deserter.

R.O.   What did your mother do during this time?

S.B.   She had to contribute to the war effort. She worked in a factory sewing and reconditioning military uniforms. I was in school for a while. Then the school was bombed, so we had to go to another school, and the last year and a half I wasn't allowed to go to school any more. Meanwhile my mother was picked up a couple of times for questioning by the Gestapo, so I was sometimes alone in the house for two or three days.

R.O.   What did you do during the months you were out of school?

S.B.   I wandered around the streets, and I was happy when there was an air raid because then I'd pick my mother up at the factory and we'd run together to the air raid shelter in the big bunker at Friedrichshain.

The end of the war was indescribably wonderful. We could walk through the streets holding our heads high and know that we wouldn't be persecuted or spat at any more. I gazed again at the people who had taunted me, though for years I had walked past them as though they didn't exist. That's what *I* did anyway: others might have done differently. And then I was really happy when I met my husband. You know with most of the men my age it was a bit dicey: it could have been someone who had been in the HJ [Hitler Youth].

My husband was born in 1929. He's five years older than I am. My husband was also born of a mixed marriage, but his mother was Christian and his father Jewish. During the war he was in Berlin with his brother, but I didn't know him then. My mother-in-law protected him the way my father protected me. You know people like that should be put on a golden throne! It's really like...I don't know whether you would find that kind of loyalty in our generation. I'd almost say you wouldn't.

According to Jewish law, Jewishness is inherited through the mother, but under Hitler's laws it was the father's background that counted. The children of a Jewish father automatically had to wear a yellow star, carry a 'J' on their identity cards, and they were fair game for anybody. Because of that, at the end of the war my husband was in particularly bad shape both physically and emotionally.

R.O.   You mentioned the HJ. Was your husband expected to join the HJ?

S.B.   No, we were lucky, we weren't allowed in. You know young people are very susceptible to organizations, and I have to tell you honestly, when I saw the girls in my neighbourhood walking down the street in their BDM [German Young Women's Organization] uniforms I was always sad that I couldn't join them, because I had no idea of the goals for which they were being mobilized. And for my husband there were only certain hours when he was allowed on the street at all.

R.O. And during this whole time was your family in the *Jüdische Gemeinde*?

S.B. My mother was, of course.

R.O. And after the war were you and your husband both recognized as Jews?

S.B. He was a Jew, but I had to convert. I had six weeks of lessons with Dr Riesenburger. It was two hours every Monday. I learned the Jewish months, a little bit of Hebrew, a couple of basic concepts, and the laws of *Kashruth*. Then they congratulated me and reinstated me in the *Jüdische Gemeinde*, and that was it. Then, when I met my husband, and we wanted to marry under the *chupa*, I had to go to the *mikveh*. I'll bet you wanted to know that!

R.O. Is there a *mikveh* here?

S.B. Yes, it's still here: it's in the Auguststrasse, near Oranienburger-strasse. I can tell you, though, that I was mad that I had to go: it's like a big bathtub, and that's also something you don't forget. We were married in 1958. Dr Riesenburger performed the ceremony, and Mr Nachama[1] sang. He was still very much a dandy then – svelte, and with fine features.

R.O. Do you keep a kosher home?

S.B. No. You know I don't want to talk about all the things I *don't* do. I am a Jew and everyone knows that, and they also knew that during the years when our children were in school. Here they say sometimes that in school you shouldn't say that you're Jewish. To the contrary, my husband has it on his identity card and the children brought it in to school so the school authorities certainly saw it. And, in fact, our children were always excused from school on the High Holidays so that they could come to Temple with us.

Our daughter Marion was born in 1959, and our sons Joachim and Detlev in 1962 and 1966. As long as Mr Ingster[2] gave lessons to the children at the *Jüdische Gemeinde* our children went, but, you know, it takes a lot of time, and Mr Ingster also had a full-time job. And at the end there were only five or six children left. But both our sons had a Bar-Mitzva.

R.O.   Did your children have any anti-Semitic experiences?

S.B.   No. None at all.

R.O.   Do your children have many Jewish friends?

S.B.   They have just about none here. Dr Kirchner's son Gerrit is exactly the age of our Detlev, and they're very happy to see each other over the High Holidays or when there's something going on at the Youth Group. But otherwise they have no contact: it's not as if they would live in the same neighbourhood.

R.O.   Do your boys have girlfriends yet?

S.B.   No, but they're looking. They're still young.

R.O.   And your daughter?

S.B.   She's about to get a divorce, thank God, and her husband wasn't Jewish. Their little girl isn't registered yet with the *Jüdische Gemeinde*, but she probably will be. Our daughter is a typesetter for the *Tribüne*;[3] one of our sons installs insulation, and the other is an electrical fitter. All three children are members of the *Jüdische Gemeinde*, but they're no Temple-goers. Though my daughter comes for the holidays.

R.O.   Are they in the Youth Group?

S.B.   The Youth Group meets at times that are a bit difficult for us. My sons work an hour away from downtown, usually on construction projects, so they come home from work late and dead tired. It would be different if they met on a weekend.

R.O.   What about the Sunday afternoon cultural programmes?

S.B.   I go, but right now the boys are busy. You know we have a little piece of land outside the city, and on weekends the boys are fixing it up.

R.O.   Which part of Berlin were you living in during the war?

S.B.   We were living in Friedrichshain, but in 1945 we were bombed out, so after the war, in '47, we got a flat in the Silbersteinstrasse in Neukölln through Galinski. My father was unemployed then and so was I. I wanted to study nursing at the hospital in Neukölln: I hoped to work in the newborn unit. I did one year as a *Praktikantin* (apprentice). Then I was thrown out because I was in the FDJ [Free German Youth] – that was in 1952 – and I came back to the eastern sector as fast as I could.

R.O.   When did you join the FDJ?

S.B.   When it was founded: I guess it was in 1946.

R.O.   Were you politicized then?

S.B. No.

R.O. How did you come in contact with the FDJ then?

S.B. Through friends.

R.O. But you were a member of the *Jüdische Gemeinde*. Was that a contradiction for you?

S.B. No, we were all in the *Jüdische Gemeinde* then and also in the FDJ.

R.O. How many of you were there?

S.B. I don't know. It only came out much later: you'd be talking with someone and you'd learn that the one or the other person had been in the FDJ. And no one said: 'Oh, you're in the FDJ.' You just did it, and you did it, naturally, with enthusiasm.

R.O. How did Galinski deal with the Jews in the FDJ?

S.B. I can't tell you anything more about Mr Galinski, but I can tell you that I came back here proudly, wearing my FDJ badge. Young people don't mind being a bit provocative.

R.O. Are you in the Party?

S.B. No.

R.O. Were you ever in the Party?

S.B. No. But I was in the FDJ, and my children were too: and also in the Pioneers. I'm not of the opinion that if I'm in the FDJ, I'm in the Party. I also don't believe that if I have a certain point of view, then I have to be in the Party. I stand behind our state 100%, and when I have something to say about what I don't like, then I'll say it to anyone, as I've always done: but I don't have to be in the Party to do that. If I would agree with the Party about everything, I'd join. But if I don't agree with everything, then I don't join.

R.O. When did you begin to work for the *Jüdische Gemeinde*?

S.B. I began to work actively with the *Gemeinde* in 1977. It was at Dr Kirchner's initiative: he needed someone to look after the Jewish citizens a bit, someone of the Jewish faith. Our citizens have already suffered enough, and he was looking for an insider, for someone with empathy. We're about 175 Jews here, of which five are already over 90 years old. I'm in charge of the senior citizens, those over 55. I write them birthday cards, and I make house visits and telephone those with health problems to see whether they need to see a doctor or need any kind of help. You know we have an institution called the *Volkssolidarität* (People's Solidarity) which sends out aides to help senior citizens in their homes. Often when a patient is discharged from hospital, the hospital will request home care, but when one of our citizens needs help I can also arrange it.

R.O. About how many hours a week do you work?

S.B. I'm paid for working 35 hours a month, but if I spend a little more time, that's also OK.

R.O. How would you like to see your work develop in the future?

S.B. Well, for my own work, if I could have an automobile available and maybe someone to work with me, then I could make the visits more easily and do a bit more for our older people, but that's a question of money, and it's not very realistic.

Professionally one naturally feels a bit boxed-in here. I'd like, for example, to see an old age home on the other side of the wall and observe how they handle their social work. I do my work not as a learned trade, but rather I try to think and feel how I would experience old age or what I as an older person would want to have available, and I let that guide me. By the way, I forgot to mention, I haven't done this work continuously since 1977. I stopped for two years when my husband came out of the hospital. He was very sick and I had to stay home with him. But, thank God, he got better, and then I started to work again.

R.O. Your husband does work similar to yours, doesn't he?

S.B. My husband is actually an electrician by trade, but for the last twelve years he's been an invalid. He has heart trouble, diabetes, and circulation problems. For five or six years, though, he's done some work for the VDN [Persecutees of the Nazi Regime]. He's in charge of ten or twelve older people there: he too looks after them a bit, congratulates them on their birthday, and makes sure that they have help when they need it.

R.O. Are there many Jews in the VDN?

S.B. All the Jews are in the VDN because the VDN is responsible for everyone who has been politically or racially persecuted.

R.O. Can you tell me a little about the *Jüdische Gemeinde* here and how it's developed over the years?

S.B. Well, Dr Kirchner has been in charge for thirteen years, and I must say that he does everything he possibly can to hold the Jews together, even though he's under a lot of pressure at work. I don't know of any other President who's accomplished as much as he has. He's created among us a feeling of belonging that no one before him knew how to organize. Before Dr Kirchner there were many Presidents, but they were much older, and they weren't too interested in the problems of the younger people. Anyway that's how I see it, though someone else might see it very differently.

For example, I would have enjoyed having a youth group here when I was younger. My husband and Dr Kirchner got to know each other through the Youth Group in the western sector, before the *Gemeinde* split in 1953. I don't know exactly what they do in our Youth Group now because we're not invited. I don't even know whether they're all members of the *Gemeinde*, but my children have found it really nice.

R.O. I was very impressed with the Sunday afternoon cultural programmes I attended last winter, and I was also impressed that so many people came.

S.B. Those people came from the churches or they're friends of Jews. Maybe 10% of the people that were sitting there are Jewish.

R.O. But the hall was full.

S.B. Yes. Sometimes we even have to leave the doors open. The cultural events at the *Gemeinde* are very good: Dr Kirchner plans them well. And people hear about them and come. I would like to see more of our older members there, but they have problems with their feet and it's always hard to get a taxi here. And even if they get a taxi to the Oranienburgerstrasse, it's hard to get a taxi to take them home. We now have many senior citizens who don't come around to the *Gemeinde* because they're too sick, but that doesn't mean they're turning away from it. Before Dr Kirchner took over, we didn't have any of these programmes: we just had prayer services on the holidays.

R.O. I know that two of the five members of the Board of Directors are women. Can you say anything more about the role of women in the *Jüdische Gemeinde* here?

S.B. Well, Frau Zuckermann who's on the Board has led the Women's Group for about twenty years. There used to be about 25 to 28 women in the group: they're now down to about eight to ten.

R.O. What do they do?

S.B. They go to the Café Moscow and drink coffee together a few times a year.

R.O. To what extent do you think your Jewishness is influenced by your experiences during the Fascist years? If there hadn't been a Hitler, do you think you would have been less Jewish?

S.B. No, probably more Jewish. It's a question of faith, of believing or not believing: and after having lived through such hard times here, it's hard to say whether I might have believed more. Perhaps yes, because then I wouldn't have experienced so much disappointment. It would also be very different to be able to come together with many more Jews. I know far too few Jews: in my age group especially there are very few of us. None of my childhood friends came back from Auschwitz. And since the division of the *Gemeinde*, we have no contact – I must say *unfortunately* – no contact with the Jews in the other sector.

I would like, however, to see that our *Gemeinde* does not become defined as a museum, but that we continue to have members – members who maintain a firm and active commitment to us and to our work.

Hermann Simon

4 The Jewish Community and the Preservation of Jewish Culture in East Berlin*

Dr Hermann Simon

Hermann Simon was born in Berlin in 1949. He studied in Prague and at Humboldt University in East Berlin where he received his PhD in History and Oriental Studies in 1974. He is currently Curator for Oriental Medieval Coins at the Staatliche Museum zu Berlin. Dr Simon is Vice-President of the East Berlin Jewish Community. He has written many articles in his field: his book, *Das Berliner Jüdische Museum in der Oranienburger Strasse*, was published by the (West) Berlin Museum in 1983.

H.S.   My parents are both Jewish: they were both members of the Jewish Community here before 1933. During the Nazi times my father fought with the Jewish Brigade in the Middle East and in Europe, and my mother was with the Communist Resistance in Berlin. After the war my father returned to Berlin, and my parents married. They are both Professors in the Department of Philosophy at Humboldt University. I was born here in 1949.

R.O.   What kind of Jewish upbringing did you have?

H.S.   A traditional one. We went to synagogue regularly, and we celebrated the holidays. I had religious instruction with Rabbi Riesenburger, and I had a Bar-Mitzva.

R.O.   Do you keep kosher?

H.S.   No.

R.O.   Are you a member of the Party?

H.S.   No.

R.O.   Have you had any anti-Semitic experiences here?

---

*A shortened form of this interview appeared in the *Journal of Jewish Communal Service*, Fall 1986.

H.S. All Jews have anti-Semitic experiences sooner or later. Here, for example, sometimes when it's too loud, people say: *'das ist ja hier wie in einer Judenschule'* (it sounds like a Jew school in here), but it's not always consciously anti-Semitic, and it shouldn't be taken overly seriously. You know, if a Jewish child has to repeat a year in school the parents are often quick to accuse the teacher of anti-Semitism and reluctant to recognize that their child might be a slow learner.

R.O. What about West Germany: have you had anti-Semitic experiences there?

H.S. Once in Cologne I saw a German harassing a Black on the street. I wouldn't say it's impossible for such a thing to happen here, but I can say that I've never seen anything comparable in the German Democratic Republic, and our state does take an unequivocal stand against anti-Semitism and against racism generally.

R.O. Your most recent book is a history of the Berlin Jewish Museum which opened in 1933 and was dissolved by the Nazis in 1938. The research and writing must have involved a significant professional and personal confrontation.

H.S. That book was a very important project for me, and for Berlin Jewish history. The people who founded the Berlin Jewish Museum and maintained it for five years under increasing pressure from the Nazis are all dead now. Their children who still read German and who are scattered throughout the world have preserved some documents and photos of the museum. But the next generation, the grandchildren, will throw these valuable sources in the waste basket unless we save them first.

The research was particularly interesting for me in a number of ways. For one thing, professionally I've always dealt with much more remote periods in history. From eight in the morning to five in the afternoon I work on medieval history, usually with coins and written documents. This kind of investigation involves a lot of reading, interpreting, and reading between the lines to try to reconstruct the reality behind the artifacts. And there's no opportunity to confront the historical actors directly: The Sasanian kings can't walk into my office and confirm or disprove my hypothesis.

When I was working on the history of the Berlin Jewish Museum, I was using pretty much the same historical methods, but you can't imagine how thrilled I was when, in January 1983, Erna Stein, Director of the Berlin Jewish Museum from 1933 to 1935, walked right into my office here on the Oranienburgerstrasse, which is just a few metres away from her old office. I recognized her immediately because she was wearing the same gold bracelet she wore in a photograph of her sitting at her desk in the museum in 1934; that was the only good photo of her from those years to survive the Nazis. She sat down, and we had a long talk about the museum: more important, she confirmed most of my impressions. Since I also work in a Berlin muscum, I have a good feel for how this kind of institution functions.

Six months later she died in Israel – she had emigrated to Palestine in 1935 – and I wrote an obituary for her that was published in our bulletin, the *Nachrichtenblatt*. From there the German press in Israel picked it up and printed it, which suggests that the people who founded the Berlin Jewish Museum have been forgotten in the countries to which they emigrated. Had I not written an obituary for this woman who was so important in Berlin Jewish history, there probably wouldn't have been any.

R.O. What is, for you, the importance of this small and short-lived Jewish museum?

H.S. First, like any other cultural institution, it offered the opportunity for recreation, aesthetic enjoyment, and intellectual stimulation. But under those historical circumstances it also served to renew the Berlin Jews' pride in the past greatness of the Jewish people and, through that, to sharpen their self-awareness and give them the hope and courage to resist the Nazi persecution. And when I say 'resist', I'm not talking about distributing flyers, exploding Molotov cocktails, or industrial sabotage. I'm thinking, rather, of a spiritual resistance – what Ernst Simon (who is not related to me) called '*Aufbau im Untergang*' (building in the midst of destruction).

R.O. Why was your book published in West Berlin and not here?

H.S. In terms of the way the book came to be written and published, you've formulated the question wrongly: I didn't write a manuscript, and then look for a publisher. I published a couple of articles on subjects related to the Berlin Jewish Museum in the *Nachrichtenblatt*: then the (West) Berlin Museum approached me. They wanted to publish something to commemorate the fiftieth anniversary of the founding of the Berlin Jewish Museum, and they asked me to write a piece for them. I agreed to write an essay, but it grew into a book.

I never offered the manuscript to any of our publishers. Had I done so, it would certainly have been accepted, but it would have taken much longer for it to appear. People are aware of the extent of the literature we publish with Jewish themes, and they also buy those books like crazy.

R.O. In West Berlin there's an initiative to rebuild the Berlin Jewish Museum. Do you feel that this is a realistic proposition in either sector of the city, or even, possibly, as a cooperative venture?

H.S. It would be impossible to rebuild the old museum simply because the objects it once housed are now scattered all over the world. But something along those lines should be done and will be done: the question is only when. I have some ideas on the subject, but I'm not yet ready to make them public.

R.O.   Is there currently a Jewish collection in the museum where you work, or in any other museum in East Berlin?

H.S.   We have a small Jewish Museum in the town of Gröbzig, but here in Berlin, the individual museums – for example, the Museum of German History – have one or another document or object of Jewish interest, but there is no permanent collection. We did have a special exhibit once, though. In 1978 the Museum of German History organized an exhibit in the foyer of the synogogue on the Rykestrasse to commemorate the fortieth anniversay of *Kristallnacht*. It was called *Vergesst es nie!* (Never forget), and it was about the persecution of the Jews in the years 1933-45 and its relationship to the Fascists' preparations for war.

R.O.   In November 1983 you attended a conference of progressive Jews from the Western German-speaking countries including, besides West Germany, Switzerland, Austria and Denmark. What were your impressions of that conference and of the people you met there?

H.S.   Well, I was a bit surprised that it was so chaotic. I can't understand why people argued for an hour over the agenda, rather than just getting on with the business. But I was a guest and it's not for me to criticize. I was also impressed and frightened by the reports about increasing neo-Nazism in West Germany. One issue that I did identify with, however, was the question of whether to work inside or independently of the established Jewish community. I think many Jews here have similar discussions, though they don't bring it up with me because my position on this matter is clear.

R.O.   You know, in the West, most Jews who consider themselves socialists are not religious, though many of them are interested in various aspects of secular Jewish culture – for example, Yiddish literature or folk music.

H.S.   You've already interviewed a woman [Jalda Rebling] who sings Yiddish songs here but who is not a member of the *Jüdische Gemeinde*. Why don't you ask her how she feels about the Jewish Community? I'm of the opinion that you have to be consistent in your convictions: you shouldn't play games with them, and you shouldn't turn them into a business. You should join the *Jüdische Gemeinde* and work with us. Especially in this country, if the Jews don't maintain their communal life, it will amount to delivering a belated victory to the Nazis – Jewish life in Berlin will simply cease to exist. But this is my very personal opinion, and it's the kind of thing each Jew has to decide for him or herself.

R.O. The extent of any individual's commitment to religious observance can have a lot to do with one's background and personal preferences. But in the West synagogues or congregations attract and maintain their membership, to a certain extent, by offering not only religious rituals, but also a variety of cultural programmes, even sports.

H.S. Look, America is very different from the German Democratic Republic, and you can't judge us by what happens there. And we do have a Youth Group, a Women's Group, a little bit of religious instruction, and regular cultural events which are good and well attended. What more can we do? The *Jüdische Gemeinde* is, naturally, first and foremost, a religious community and not a cultural association.

R.O. What happens when people do apply to join the *Jüdische Gemeinde*? What do they have to do?

H.S. There is no easy answer to that question because the decision to admit someone to the Jewish Community is made by a Rabbi and not by the Board of Directors. Since we have no Rabbi, Rabbi Stein[1] usually handles this, though he would never go against our wishes. The problem is basically one of evaluating the sincerity of the application, and it's very hard to generalize. We usually invite the applicant to talk with us at least two or three times, and then we judge each case individually.

R.O. Could you describe a concrete case of an application for membership and how it developed?

H.S. We're such a small community here that it would be impossible to talk about an actual case without breaching the confidence involved in such a personal procedure. And, besides, once we have accepted someone into the Jewish Community, he or she is considered a Jew like the rest of us, and we would never single him or her out as a newcomer. I can tell you, though, that the people who have the hardest time are those who come to us and say: 'I just saw this movie, and what was done to the Jews was so terrible, and I was so moved that I want to be a Jew too.' We have the least patience with them.

R.O. How many applications for membership do you handle every year?

H.S. In most cases the initiatives never reach the stage of becoming formal applications. What happens is that someone new will start coming around to services, or on Sunday afternoons. We then invite the person to talk to us, and we suggest that he or she join the Youth Group: if it's a man, we make it clear that at some point he will be expected to undergo circumcision. This fall we're preparing to accept two women into the *Gemeinde*.

R.O. What do they have to do?

H.S. They have to demonstrate their knowledge of Judaism. That is, they have to be able to read Hebrew, they have to know about the holidays, and they basically have to be able to articulate their reasons for wanting to come to us.

R.O. What about the *mikveh*?

H.S. We have a *mikveh* here, but it needs repair, so the Rabbi will have to make a decision. If he says it's not necessary, no one here will challenge him, but my own opinion is that if we're going to do this, we should do a proper and complete job.

R.O. Does the Jewish Community here have any special projects or new programmes on its agenda?

H.S. We've just finished putting up a new wall around our cemetery at Weissensee. It cost 2.5 million [East German] marks, and there's already a rumour going around that it was paid for by a rich Jewish woman in America. In fact, it was paid for by the Magistrate of the City of (East) Berlin, and the money came from the fund for residential construction. That means they'll build a couple of flats fewer this year.

And that reminds me that we have received complaints from visitors to our city about the condition of the Jewish cemeteries here: namely, that they're overgrown and that the graves are not cared for regularly. I'd like to answer by reminding those who are interested that the Weissensee cemetery is the largest Jewish cemetery in Europe: it has almost 115 000 graves. In the early 1930s it was maintained by 150 full-time employees. Today there are fewer than 200 members of the Jewish Community here. In other words, we've inherited a treasure that is far beyond our administrative capacity: but we do the best we can, and the state and city support our efforts.

R.O. You've just taken over leadership of the *Jüdische Gemeinde's* Youth Group. Could you say something about what's happening there?

H.S. I was appointed leader of the Youth Group two months ago, and I don't have any firm ideas yet about future programming. Right now I'm trying to get the young people to express their ideas about what they'd like to do. We are planning trips to see plays and films of Jewish interest. It's been suggested that we visit the Jewish Community in Prague: we now have to find out whether we can arrange it. In the past we've organized excursions to the Jewish Museum in Gröbzig, and to a former farm in Stickelsdorf where, until 1938, the German Zionist Youth used to prepare themselves for emigration to Palestine.

R.O. What other projects would you like to see the *Jüdische Gemeinde* here undertake in the future?

H.S. Well, one thing we'll have to deal with is the ruin next door that used to be the synagogue on the Oranienburgerstrasse.[2] Sooner or later we'll have to rebuild it – even as a ruin, it's expensive to keep it from becoming dangerous – and the money will have to come from somewhere. I would also like to see our bulletin, the *Nachrichtenblatt*, upgraded. We have plenty of space there, and we can publish quickly. There's more than one opinion about this, but I think we should have more intellectual content – for example, more reviews of new books, films, plays, etc. Also 1986 will be the 200th anniversary of the death of Moses Mendelssohn, and something should definitely be done about that, perhaps a special issue of the *Nachrichtenblatt*.

R.O. Moses Mendelssohn was a secular Jew and a capitalist.

H.S. But most important, is that he stood for enlightenment, religious tolerance, and for the Jewish contribution to Berlin's evolution from a small town to the great economic and cultural centre it later became.

R.O. Is there anything else you'd like to bring up?

H.S. I know that many Jews in the English-speaking countries emigrated from – or come from families that used to live in – the Berlin area. I've tried to mention some of the sights here of Jewish interest, and I hope that when Jews travel to West Berlin, they'll think of visiting the German Democratic Republic too.

Irene Runge

5 A Newcomer to the Jewish Community*
Dr Irene Runge

Irene Runge was born in 1942 in Washington Heights in New York City. In 1949 she moved with her parents to the German Democratic Republic. She received her PhD in Economics and Sociology in 1979 from Humboldt University where she is currently a Researcher in the Department of History. Dr Runge is serving her first term on the Board of Directors of East Berlin's Jewish Community. A regular contributor to *Sonntag*, a cultural and political weekly newspaper, and to the literary magazine *Temperamente* (both in East Berlin), she has also written two books: *Älter werden-alt sein* (Dietz Verlag, East Berlin, 1982), and *Ganz in Familie* (Dietz Verlag, East Berlin, 1985).

I.R. My father came from a religious Jewish family; my mother was originally non-Jewish, but she converted. My parents were married by a Rabbi in Palestine in the 1930s. They had left Germany already in 1929, and they were also in Paris for several years. Then, when France was invaded, they went to the United States where they lived from 1939 to 1949. So I was born in New York. My father, a writer and art historian, had a book and picture shop in Times Square, down in the subway station, and he also served as secretary of the exiled German writers association. He used to organize exhibitions and other cultural events – many of them took place at the New School building on 14th Street – to help make progressive German artists and writers known in North America.

Our family returned to Germany in 1949. My parents were politically disappointed in New York. It was the McCarthy era, and many of their friends were going back to Germany because they had political problems or feared they might get into trouble. At this time also the German Democratic Republic was being founded in the Soviet-occupied Zone, so there were opportunities for returning emigrés to take part in reconstructing a new and better Germany. For the first year we lived in Leipzig. Then in 1950 we moved to Berlin where my father worked in the Ministry of Information. For many years he produced radio programmes and published

*A shortened version of this interview appeared in *Response*, Summer – Fall 1986.

a magazine for them. Later he worked freelance, translating American literature and writing.

R.O.   What was it like to move to Germany as a seven-year old?

I.R.   In a way, when I first came here, I didn't really come to Germany because the people I met had all just gotten back too, and the children I played with were, naturally, the children of these returning emigrants. I don't even know when I first came into contact with normal Germans. We had a maid, but I didn't have much to do with other ordinary Germans till quite a bit later. In 1951 my mother died, and we changed apartments three or four times. I picked up German very quickly, but I was still very American. At the beginning I wore blue jeans and T-shirts. I never had long braids like the German girls had, and I never wore those long brown stockings. The German kids didn't understand that, and their parents didn't either. Then after a while, I wasn't allowed to wear jeans any more because they said it was American imperialist culture, and we shouldn't have any contact with that. I also didn't know how to behave: I couldn't cut meat with a knife, and I couldn't sit quietly, so I always got bad grades in school.

R.O.   You mentioned in your autobiographical short story[1] that school-mates used to ask you whether you killed Jesus.

I.R.   Yes, that's something I remember because I didn't really understand it then. I asked my father and other people what that meant, and they just told me not to play with those kids any more. This was in 1951, and the children probably didn't really know what Jews are, but they may have heard from their parents that all these Jewish people were coming back.

R.O.   Did you have any kind of Jewish home life?

I.R.   Only very indirectly. In those days it was pretty tough to get meat, and my father never liked pork, so our friends brought us all kinds of recipes for preparing pork so that it tastes like chicken. My father also used to always wear a hat. It was never really said that it had something to do with being Jewish: they said it was just because of the draft. And, naturally, we knew a lot of people who came from concentration camps: people would often talk about those days and what they experienced in the camps. I didn't realize till much later that that's not Germany, but a special social and political culture. Also we always had guests, and there were always parties going on: my parents and their friends needed to be together. That was very unusual in those days: normal Germans had birthday parties and that was it.

We never really had any Christmas. My father bought a Christmas tree because he thought I needed it to be assimilated, but the way he did it never made me like it. But, you know, in that story I never mention the word 'Jew' or being Jewish: I just wanted to describe that returned emigrant culture at that point in history. Still, all of my Jewish friends and acquaintances who read the story identified with it. The Germans who read it asked me a lot of questions because they didn't understand it.

After my mother died I had more contact with ordinary Germans. Their apartments were different from ours: they had less space than we did, but still they always had a *wohnzimmer*, a good room where they usually didn't sit. When I would ring the doorbell to ask whether a friend could come out and play, they would never invite me into the flat like our friends did, but they made me wait for my friend outside. And then – something I wrote about in that story – they had pictures of their families: an uncle, brother, or cousin in uniform, German uniform. But I was brought up to think of men in German uniforms as the enemy. They had relatives: they had their family around them, and we didn't have anybody. So the whole German family hierarchy didn't play for us the organizing role it assumed in a normal German family. For us, our friends and comrades who also came back from emigration substituted for the extended family.

I had lots of problems in school. Our family's social circle consisted mostly of writers, intellectuals – very bright people. The teachers in school were very rigid and not so bright. We would read a novel in school, and the teacher would explain what the author meant. I would raise my hand and say: 'But I talked to the author yesterday, and he said he never meant that'. Then the teacher would reprimand me for raising negative and provocative questions. But I was brought up to think I should have my own opinion because every opinion is valuable.

The other thing is that when I was seventeen, I had a boyfriend. This was quite unusual – in those days you weren't supposed to have an affair while you were still in school – and it distracted me from my school work. I was also having a lot of trouble with my father at that time. He had remarried and I didn't get along very well with his wife. And he really didn't have that much time to care because he was always with his books. So in 1959 I dropped out of school, and moved out of their place. Then I got married, had a child a few months later, and then got divorced. This happened to a lot of women I know, but in most cases after the women had finished school and started at university, or even later.

R.O. Was your first husband Jewish?

I.R. No. But the problem was not that he wasn't Jewish, but rather this was the first time that I got involved with a real German family with relatives in the West and no anti-Fascist background. I was very suspicious of them: I couldn't accept the fact that they had a family and I didn't, and I just couldn't manage. So I tried to force my husband not to have any contact with his parents. Naturally, he went there secretly. When I found out about it, I got very upset, and the whole thing broke up.

After I dropped out of school, I worked for the press agency and the radio. For the most part I did filing and other unskilled clerical work, but I also did some writing, and sometimes I worked as an interpreter. I had always wanted to be a writer: everyone I knew was an intellectual, and I didn't even know what else one could do. But I also knew that I needed a few years to goof off.

R.O.   Who was taking care of your baby during those years?

I.R.   Since I was working, my former mother-in-law took Stefan during the week. She didn't have a job, and she and her husband had a nice little house in the suburbs. That was a good environment for Stefan, and on Fridays I picked him up, and he was with me for the weekend. It was a pretty good arrangement.

R.O.   And how did you get these various jobs that you had?

I.R.   That was no problem. Many of the people we knew were in leading positions and it was no problem for them to give me a job for a couple of years.

R.O.   Were you in the Socialist Unity Party or in any other political party at this time?

I.R.   No. I wasn't disciplined enough.

I met my current husband Heinz in 1967. He isn't Jewish either: he's Protestant, and he doesn't want to convert, but he comes with me to all the cultural events at the Jewish Community. He's an opera director and he knew lots of Jews professionally even before he met me, so it's really quite comfortable. Around this time I also went back to school. I got my *Abitur* (the German pre-university degree) in 1971, and then I studied economics and sociology at university.

R.O.   During your early years did you and your family have any relationship with the Jewish Community here?

I.R.   No. Most of our friends and acquaintances were Jewish, but none of them were religious. We talked a lot about being Jewish and we told Jewish jokes, but the *Jüdische Gemeinde* seemed to be very religious, and we had no contact with it because our people weren't members. Then, in the early 1970s, a friend of mine became a member: she came to the GDR from Australia. She grew up there in a religious family and had been a member of the Communist Party in Australia. She also had difficulty when she got here because she was much older and she really didn't know how to integrate, so she became a member of the *Jüdische*

Gemeinde. Through contact with her I also began to think that if you're Jewish, it makes sense to really identify as a Jew and to do more about it: though I never was a very religious Jew. I think I would probably be a Reform Jew in the United States.

First I started going to the cultural Sundays we have here and my friend took me to a Seder. Somewhat later I began to attend services at the synagogue and I found out that they're not really very friendly there.

R.O.   What do you mean by that?

I.R.   Well, if they don't know you, they don't really welcome you that openly. That's very German.

R.O.   And that didn't put you off?

I.R.   No, because I knew people there. Hermann Simon and I went to university together, and I knew other people who were already members. This made it easier for me; and so in 1976 I too became a member.

R.O.   Did you give your son any kind of Jewish upbringing?

I.R.   Not really, because he was brought up mostly by his non-Jewish grandparents. But, from the beginning, he knew that there was a difference – that his parents moved in very different social worlds. And, as he got older, he tended to be more interested in our family. When Stefan was fifteen or so, I started taking him to synagogue. Naturally he didn't like it: he didn't understand a word and he didn't know what was going on. But then he joined the Youth Group, and he liked that. Ultimately he decided that he wanted to become Jewish, so he got circumcised, he learned Hebrew, and at a late age, he had a Bar-Mitzva; now he's also a member of the Jewish Community. He got married last winter. His wife Katrin is pregnant, and she just applied to become a member too so that the baby can grow up as a Jew. They're both reading a lot of books about Judaism; they made Seders for Passover this year, and they're really trying to make a Jewish home.

R.O.   What does Katrin have to do to convert?

I.R.   I think she has to learn some Hebrew and have a Bar-Mitzva. One problem is that our *mikveh* doesn't work, and there's no point in spending lots of money to reconstruct it if we'll only use it once a year at most. So the question is whether we'll use the *mikveh* in Prague, or the one in Budapest, or maybe a river. Hermann is working on this with Rabbi Stein who will probably officiate.

R.O.   You've been on the board of Directors of the *Jüdische Gemeinde* for a year. What do you feel are the major problems that the Jewish Community here is now facing?

I.R.   One very important problem is defining who is Jewish. The Jewish laws regarding this issue are very different from the Nuremberg Laws,[2] and a lot of people fall in between the two. For example, people with a Jewish father or a Jewish grandfather were persecuted as Jews by the Fascists, and hence they and their children feel that they are Jewish – or at least partly Jewish. People like this apply to join the *Gemeinde*, and the *Gemeinde* tells them that they're not Jewish because you're only Jewish if you have a Jewish mother. I think the Jewish Community isn't aware of how many people there are in this group. Such people feel they have no roots in German culture. Though they didn't have a traditional Jewish upbringing, they would like to be more Jewish. So they come around on Sunday afternoons, and ask to join the *Gemeinde*. But the *Gemeinde* really gives them a tough time. They have to prove that they're very serious and they have to have a proper conversion. When people who feel that they're Jewish get turned away by the *Gemeinde* on the basis of Jewish law, they feel rejected, confused, and hurt: and usually they drift away again.

You also have to keep in mind that our Jewish Community isn't just one congregation, it's the only Jewish organization we have. We have no Reform Jewish Community. So it seems to me quite clear that sticking to this very conservative definition of Jewishness will lead to our organizational death. Many of our members are very old, and can't come to services any more. It's already difficult to get a *minyan* together here, but somehow we manage – there are some kids who come and visitors who come over from the West. In the rest of the GDR they never have a *minyan*; I've heard that they have to get Jewish Palestinians in. And they don't count women either.

R.O.   There are rumours about initiatives to reconstitute here the Berlin Jewish Museum that the Nazis dissolved in 1938. Do you know anything about that?

I.R.   I know a woman who was interested in having a Jewish museum again. She got a lot of Jewish people who are not members of the Jewish Community interested, but the Jewish Community didn't like the idea too much. We don't have personnel with the knowledge to maintain a Jewish museum. And then come all the technical questions like, where would we get things to exhibit, and who would pay for it?

What I would like to see is something a bit different. There's talk about one day reconstructing the synagogue on the Oranienburgerstrasse. We already have a beautifully reconstructed synagogue which we can't fill on the Rykestrasse, so we certainly don't need another one. But we could reconstruct the façade of the Oranienburgerstrasse synagogue and make it into a cultural centre. We could have a permanent exhibition and move our Jewish library there. We could also use the building for meetings, for showing films; people who do research on the Holocaust or on Berlin Jewish history could work there. In the years before 1933, Berlin was a major centre of Jewish life, and Oranienburgerstrasse is a historic street. I don't think we should wait until the city decides what to do with the ruin; we should tell them what to do. You know that synagogue was the building where Reform Judaism began and maybe, with the help of Jews all over the world who are interested in Berlin and might make donations, we could again have some very exciting things going on there. That's my personal idea, though; I don't know whether the Jewish Community likes it.

R.O. In 1987 the City of Berlin will be celebrating the 750th anniversary of its founding. Will the Jewish Community be taking part in any of the public ceremonies to mark the event?

I.R. I don't know that any plans have been made yet, but a cultural centre like the one I just described could be part of it. And, you know, 1986 will be the 200th anniversary of the death of Moses Mendelssohn and we could do something about that too. Unfortunately our Jewish Community is a bunch of very old people, and a lot of them are not academic people, so we can't do it all ourselves. But, as an institution, we can try to encourage other people to do some of the work, and I think we should. We should talk more about these things and be more active in public. This is part of German history and I think it's also part of the Party line here. We spent a lot of money on Martin Luther Year in 1983. Moses Mendelssohn wasn't that important for German history, but the Jews were important for German history, and we have to make that clear. Books about the synagogues here,[3] and the *Scheunenviertel*[4] – even Hermann Simon's book – have been published in West Berlin, but I think that's really something that we have to do.

Another case in point concerns the two memorials for the Herbert Baum Group[5]. The inscription on the memorial at the Jewish cemetery says that it was a group of young Jewish Communists, but the word 'Jewish' is missing from the memorial at Marx-Engels Platz, and now that the memorial is there, they won't change it. I think we ourselves have to point out publicly what it means to be Jewish in East Germany today.

R.O. Have you brought up any of these ideas for discussion at meetings of the Board of Directors?

I.R. I've only been on the Board for a year. The meetings are once every six weeks, and some of these ideas have only recently evolved in my own mind. But I've talked to some people and there is interest. I think the times are ripe for rethinking these issues, and the discussions will take place.

R.O. Could you explain a bit about the research you've done on ageing in the GDR for your book *Älter werden-alt sein* (Growing Older, Being Old)?

I.R. It's actually a pretty academic and theoretical book about the social aspects of ageing. Once I had started the project, I realized that I was doing it largely to overcome my inhibitions about getting close to older Germans. In the end, though, I didn't succeed in talking to them or getting close to them. So I let other people do that, and I got involved with the older Jews and anti-Fascists. I interviewed people who were active in the anti-Fascist movement or had been in jail or in concentration camps during the Nazi times, and I wrote about them. I wanted to make these people better known personally, and I wanted to explore the theme of what motivated these people to resist. I felt I had to show that there was a way to resist and that life does have moral content. And it wasn't only the Jewish variable: I was also interested in non-Jewish resistance fighters. And I found out that there was a lot of passive resistance in Berlin, especially among workers. Many Jews attributed their survival to the help of non-Jews who gave them food or warned them of impending danger. Some of the pieces I wrote have been published in *Sonntag*, particularly in their annual special issue for September 10 – our National Day of Anti-Fascism.

These anti-Fascists are pretty old now, but they're still very active and very politically involved. They go around to the schools and kindergartens to talk to the young people. They give presentations about Fascism, and they provide an example of the kind of personality you should develop to be important to your country or your people. This includes getting involved in all kinds of neighbourhood projects, and also opposing things that they don't like.

R.O. And what about the Germans who weren't part of the Resistance?

I.R. Well, many of the real Nazis fled to the West because they were afraid of the Russians. Those who were uninvolved or maybe little Nazi functionaries stayed and rebuilt this country, perhaps as a kind of personal *Wiedergutmachung* [restitution]. There was a lot of work to be done, and we didn't import foreign labour.

R.O. And how did these people react to you as a Jew?

I.R. Well, there is guilt and repression. When they were children they knew Jewish people; and then there were no Jewish people. When they heard I'm Jewish, they were shocked and didn't know how to behave. They didn't know what to ask me. It's something that's very complicated for them to deal with. For them being Jewish is associated with the distant past.

R.O. Have you ever had any anti-Semitic experiences here?

I.R. There's no serious anti-Semitism here, but that doesn't mean you would never find an anti-Semite. In the GDR anti-Semitism and what happened under the Nazis is discussed thoroughly in the schools. The class is taken to visit a former concentration camp, and it's made very clear what anti-Semitism and Fascism are, and that they're not acceptable. But many Germans who were born after the war understand that as something very abstract and remote, and don't relate it to the world around them. So there are lots of dirty jokes going around about Turkish people, Poles, Blacks, Africans, and Arabs. And if you point out to them that those are the same jokes that their parents and grandparents told about Jews, they look at you, and admit that it's something they never thought of.

R.O. In the last two years you visited New York City twice. Would you like to say something about your impressions and your experiences there?

I.R. I really loved and felt very close to New York. I went to see the apartment where we lived until 1949, and I met my former neighbours: that was a very moving experience for me. And then I found my family over there: people I'm related to, who look like me, and who remember me when I was a baby. That never happened to me here. New Yorkers seem very friendly and very curious, but often badly informed. Most of the people I met there were Jewish and very bright. Many people told me they don't like Germans: they talked a lot about anti-Semitism and neo-Nazis, and they told me that they don't buy German products and don't want to visit Germany. I would tell them that I don't live in West Germany, but in the German Democratic Republic which is different. Then they would ask me whether that has something to do with Moscow and with eternal evil, and whether I'm a defector. I explained that our President Erich Honecker was in jail during the Fascist times, and many people in leading positions in our country are Jewish, and others were in concentration camps or were refugees from the Nazis. And they were surprised because they had never thought of that. I also made it clear that I plan to continue living in the GDR; we do have a lot of political problems, but we also have a very strong anti-Fascist tradition starting with the founding of our state. And many people said that now that they know me, they want to find out more about the German Democratic Republic and to come visit and see what's happening here.

AUTUMN 1987

Irene Runge's daughter-in-law Katrin never joined the Jewish Community: a few months after the interview the marriage broke up. As the baby, a girl, is now living with her mother, it is unlikely that she will have a

Jewish upbringing. This all-too-common pattern among younger Jews in East Berlin in fact reproduces the non-Jewish upbringing of Dr Runge's own son Stefan.

In 1986 Dr Runge's book about the city where she was born, *Himmelhölle Manhattan* (Heaven–Hell Manhattan), was published in East Berlin by Buchverlag Der Morgen.

More important, in early 1986 Dr Runge compiled a list of fifty people she knows who come from Jewish families outside the Jewish Community who might be interested in establishing contact with the *Jüdische Gemeinde* and eventually joining. The Jewish Community invited these people to a meeting in early May 1986. The meeting was well attended and interest in a relationship with the Jewish Community was expressed. This group met a few times in 1986-87; and since September 1987 it has been meeting regularly once or twice a month. A children's group has been started, Jewish holidays are observed, and a series of lectures and discussions has been set up. Thus far only a few members of this group have applied to join the *Jüdische Gemeinde*; but there is now an interested Jewish public around the Jewish Community, and it consists largely of writers, intellectuals and artists whose ideas find their way into the political culture of the East German state. (See also Postscript, pp. 149–54).

Gerrit Kirchner

6 Jewish Education and the Jewish Youth in East Berlin

Gerrit Kirchner

Gerrit Kirchner was born in East Berlin in 1966 and has grown up as a member of East Berlin's Jewish Community, of which his father, Dr Peter Kirchner, has been President since 1971. Gerrit Kirchner received his *Abitur* (the German pre-university degree) in 1984. He is currently fulfilling his military service after which he plans to study medicine. Gerrit Kirchner has been active for several years in East Berlin's Jewish Youth Group which is the Jewish Community's programme for its younger members and for prospective members.

R.O.   What kind of Jewish education did you have as a child in East Berlin?

G.K.   During my early years at school, our Cantor, Öljean Ingster, gave Hebrew lessons to the children in the *Jüdische Gemeinde*, and I was one of those who attended. Later, a student from Israel who had married a woman in the *Gemeinde* took over the Hebrew instruction for a year or so, but then the lessons stopped. This was Hebrew language instruction exclusively: there was never any religious education. Everything I know about religion I read on my own. Cantor Estrongo Nachama from West Berlin helped me prepare for my Bar-Mitzva, and he officiated at the ceremony.

R.O.   Why was Jewish education here limited to the Hebrew language? Was the exclusion of religious instruction a political or ideological issue, or did it have to do with something else?

G.K.   This was ten years ago. Our Jewish Community never attempted to set up a real Hebrew school of the kind you have in the West. It would have been unrealistic because Cantor Ingster had a full-time job in addition to his religious duties, and he didn't have the time to take on too much more. So he simply tried to teach the children in the Jewish Community to read Hebrew – it was never taught as a spoken language – so they could follow the services in their prayer books. We used an elementary textbook from America.

R.O. How many members does the Youth Group have, and how old are they?

G.K. There are about 15 to 20 of us, and we're between the ages of 15 and 35 years old. But in my age group – 15 to 20 years old – there are only three or four. We meet on the second Tuesday evening of every month and we have a room in the Jewish Community house set aside for our use. Hermann Simon, the Vice-President of the *Jüdische Gemeinde*, leads the Youth Group, but there's no highly organized or rigid programme. The idea is, rather, to meet regularly and talk about all kinds of things. We plan events and make decisions fairly democratically: members of the group make suggestions about the kinds of things they'd like to do. Hermann Simon's function is mostly administrative. Often we invite a speaker to talk on a Jewish theme, either religious or cultural.

R.O. Do you ever have reports or discussions about Israel?

G.K. Israel comes up a lot in informal conversations, and sometimes in the course of a presentation to the group, but we don't sponsor debates about Israel or Israeli policies, and we don't take a public position on things that happen in the Middle East.

Two years ago we took a trip with young people from other Jewish Communities in the German Democratic Republic to the town of Gröbzig where there's an old, well-kept Jewish cemetery and a small Jewish Museum. Since then we haven't maintained regular contact with youth groups in the other Jewish Communities, but we're thinking of inviting them to get together with us again, maybe around the time of the High Holidays because in some cities they don't hold religious services. The League of Jewish Communities in the GDR owns a summer camp on the Baltic Coast and we could use that for larger gatherings too. Another idea we're working on is a trip to Prague to visit the Jewish Community and meet with the Jewish Youth Group there.

R.O. The Youth Group here consists of younger members of the *Jüdische Gemeinde*, and also prospective members.

G.K. Yes. The prospective members are mostly children or grandchildren of people who were Jewish but were not affiliated with the Jewish Community: in other words, people of Jewish ancestry who've had no Jewish upbringing. At some point these people began to take an interest in their Jewish heritage and to think about joining the *Jüdische Gemeinde*. But one of our conditions is that an individual who joins us should have a Jewish parent, or at least a Jewish grandparent. This is in contrast to the policy of the Protestant and Catholic youth groups here, where the atmosphere is much more open and anyone at all can come and participate.

R.O. How many members of the Youth Group are married?

G.K. Only two, and they are married to each other. The rest of us are single.

R.O. Is the Youth Group growing larger or smaller?

G.K. The size of the group is pretty stable. For the most part it's people like Hermann Simon and his sister Bettina who've grown up in the *Jüdische Gemeinde*, or people who converted to Judaism years ago. Once in a while someone brings a friend or acquaintance we've never seen before, but there's no steady stream of new faces.

R.O. Do you have any contact with young Jews in West Berlin?

G.K. Once, about nine or ten years ago, a group of Jewish young people from West Berlin came to visit us and we talked with them. The problem is that the Jewish Community in West Berlin is not interested in having contact with us or in cooperating with us in any way. In fact, I don't think they even know that there is a Youth Group here. More often, individual visitors to the city come by the Jewish Community house or look at our synagogue and cemeteries and ask us a few questions about Jewish life here. But they never think to ask about younger Jews. We would very much like to meet and have contact with other Jewish Youth Groups from socialist and from capitalist countries, but they have to be ready to have contact with us too, and sometimes to take the initiative. It would also be nice to see more younger people at our prayer services, but that depends on our members themselves.

AUTUMN 1987

The Youth Group is now meeting less regularly and some members have left. Its function has been taken over by the larger and more dynamic group started by Irene Runge (see p. 52). Several members of the Youth Group also attend events organized by the new group. In early November 1987 Gerrit Kirchner invited members of the West Berlin Jewish Students Association to Friday evening services and dinner with members of the Youth Group and younger members of Irene Runge's group. The evening proved successful and more events of this kind are being planned.

II
The Jews in the Party: The Quality of Their Jewishness and Their View of the Jewish Community

Jalda Rebling

7 A Yiddish Folksinger in the Bosom of the Party*
Jalda Rebling

Jalda Rebling was born in Amsterdam in 1951 and moved with her parents and older sister to (East) Berlin in 1952. She studied acting at the Staatliche Schauspielschule in (East) Berlin, and she has been associated with the Maxim Gorki Theatre in (East) Berlin, the Altenburg Theatre, the Städtisches Theatre in Karl-Marx-Stadt, and the Staatstheater in Dresden. In recent years Jalda Rebling has worked as a freelance actress and folksinger, specializing in Yiddish folksongs. Her record 'Für Anne Frank', produced with her parents Lin Jaldati and Eberhard Rebling, was released in (East) Berlin in 1980.

R.O. You know, my first contact with Jews and Jewish culture in the German Democratic Republic was the concert series your mother gave in Toronto in 1979. I remember your mother as being a very special person. Would you like to start by saying something about her?

J.R. Actually my parents just finished writing the first part of their combined autobiography. It's in the form of letters to their grandchildren and it should appear shortly. It will probably be called *Unser Erstes Leben* (Our First Life), and it will be published by Buchverlag der Morgen. My mother Lin Jaldati was born in 1912, and grew up in a large and warm *mischpoche* (family) in the Jewish quarter of Amsterdam as Rebecca Brillenslijper. Her father, whom I never met, almost but never quite made a living through a series of unsuccessful businesses: he sold – at different times – fish, fruit, gloves (sometimes only the left hand), and similar commodities. Therefore when my mother was fourteen years old she had to go to work in a factory, and – against her father's wishes – she began to study dancing at night. She soon began to sing and dance with a Jewish theatre company – the Anski Theatre – and, by the 1930s she was making quite a bit of money by dancing in musical shows. Starting in the mid-1930s she participated in the first concerts organized in Amsterdam to protest against what was happening in Germany and to express solidarity with the German emigrants. In 1936 Lin Jaldati (as my mother was now called) joined the Communist Party in Holland, and in

*A shortened version of this interview appeared in *Jewish Currents*, December 1986.

1937 she met my father Eberhard Rebling, a German musicologist and pianist who had left Germany in 1936, though, being neither a Communist nor a Jew, he could have easily stayed on.

At this time Lin and Eberhard were living in a communal household with several other young progressive artists, and when the Germans invaded Holland in May 1940, they all decided as a group to work with the Resistance. They served largely as couriers, obtaining and distributing false identification papers and ration cards – in fact, people Lin and Eberhard no longer recognize still come up to us after concerts to thank my parents again for having helped them escape the Nazis. At this time Lin also gave illegal concerts of Yiddish folksongs. My father encouraged and accompanied her in these concerts, though the songs she sang had nothing to do with the music he had studied at university.

In the summer of 1944 the house in which Lin and Eberhard were living was raided – presumably they were betrayed. Lin was deported with her parents, brother and sister to Westerbork, Auschwitz, and Bergen Belsen concentration camps: most of her family died in Auschwitz. Eberhard was captured, tried and sentenced to death as a German deserter, but with the help of my mother's sister he managed to escape. And my older sister Kathinka, who was at this time three years old, was spirited away by friends hours before the Gestapo came to pick her up as a hostage.

By some miracle Mama, Papa, and Kathinka all survived the war and found each other again in 1945. For a long time Mama was very sick, but as soon as she regained her strength, she began to sing again in public. In the late 1940s she gave concerts in Scandinavia and in many of the Soviet-occupied areas of Europe; she performed mostly songs of the Resistance that she had learned in the camps and Yiddish songs. In 1952, when I was a year old, the family moved to the German Democratic Republic. Mama has since broadened her repertoire to include folksongs of many countries and songs of German composers like Eisler and Dessau – both Jews. Lin is now in her seventies, but she's still a high-energy performer; she still gives concerts all over the GDR and all over the world – now with the whole *mischpoche*. It has always been very important for us to make it clear to people that there are now two Germanies, and that in the Germany where we live, the GDR, we're doing everything possible to make sure that what happened here in the 1930s can never happen again.

R.O. As the daughter of Resistance fighters who returned to commit their lives to building a socialist, anti-Fascist state in Germany, you must have had a very special kind of childhood here.

J.R. No, not at all. I had a normal childhood. The only thing that was unusual was that we spoke Dutch at home and we have very close ties to Holland. Mama and her sister – the only other member of her family who survived the war – telephone each other at least once a week, and when someone in the family is sick – if, God forbid, one of the grandchildren has the sniffles – they have to telephone each other every day to agree on the best medicine.

But apart from that, I grew up as a completely normal girl. What was different was that I was always confronted with the fate of people – logically, those in my parents' social world – who had been active in the Resistance, and so, as a child, I had no clear idea of the situation of people who had no opportunity to resist Fascism. It was only much later that I began to understand how ordinary Germans lived in Germany.

R.O. So then your early feelings of being Jewish and being a citizen of the GDR began with the Resistance?

J.R. No, I've never felt that I was particularly Jewish or non-Jewish or Dutch or non-Dutch, but just that I'm a normal person. I had the usual growing pains, and I was an average student at school, though perhaps a bit better at languages than the others.

And, you know, there is now a generation in the GDR – that is, my children – for whom it is self-understood that no one asks: 'Are you Jewish or non-Jewish, or what are you? Do you have yellow skin or black skin, and where do you come from?' Our children just play with each other and accept each other.

R.O. Yes, but you just said that your parents moved in a social world of people who had fought together in the Resistance and that you grew up in that environment. Were your childhood friends children of Resistance fighters or ordinary Germans?

J.R. Well, not completely ordinary people. You know, as a four-, five-, eight-, or nine-year-old, I never thought about it, which means, I guess, that the problem wasn't acute. It first became a problem for me later, when I was 18, 19, 20, and I left my parents' house and began to think about other people's development processes. But that's been a problem for the post-war generation for some time – who was your father, and who was my father?

R.O. Have you ever had any anti-Semitic experiences?

J.R. Once, when I was fifteen or sixteen, I was insulted by a Polish boy. Otherwise the only thing I can remember is that during my childhood we lived in Eichwalde near Berlin. Every once in a while we would find a swastika painted on our mailbox, but that was directed, naturally, at Jews and Communists – that was before 1961.[1] And sometimes we got anonymous telephone calls. But these are childhood memories, and they didn't really bother me too much because Mama and Father always explained: 'It's not so bad. These people are dangerous, but they'll never succeed.'

R.O. Progressive Jewish intellectuals in North America and West Germany often discuss the relationship between socialism and Jewishness – in what respects they are compatible, and where there are problems or contradictions. In the course of these reflections one begins to think about the role of the Jewish Community. I know that you're *not* a member of the (East) Berlin *Jüdische Gemeinde*.

J.R. No, but I have a very close relationship to the *Gemeinde*.

R.O. I remember I first met you when you gave a concert there. Could you explain a bit about why you're not a member, what kind of relationship you have with the *Gemeinde*, and how you feel about it?

J.R. Maybe I should start explaining it another way. As Mama always said, that I'm Jewish is a fact: I'm not ashamed of it, and I'm also not particularly proud of it, that's just the way it is. That being Jewish means being part of a particular cultural history is also clear. If I had been born to a Chilean mother or to a Chinese mother, then I would have grown up in another culture. But Jewishness is the culture into which I was born, and for me it mediates my thinking and coming to terms with the basic questions of heaven and earth, life and death, war and peace, and how one survives in this world at all.

I grew up in a Communist household, and I grew up as a non-believer. Actually I do believe: as Mama says, I believe in Humanity. In that sense I'm a believer, I believe we should obey the ten commandments, and this belief is an important part of our culture. And, although I'm not a member of the *Jüdische Gemeinde*, I do what I can for them.

R.O. What do you mean by that?

J.R. Well, usually I do only complete concerts. I won't just show up at an event and do two or three Yiddish songs like some kind of exotic bird. But I make an exception for the *Jüdische Gemeinde*. If Eugen Gollomb[2] asks me to come to Leipzig and sing a couple of songs at their Chanuka party, I don't refuse.

R.O. Do you give your children a Jewish upbringing?

J.R. No, I'm not giving them a special Jewish upbringing. I have two sons, Jacob and Tobias – both uncircumcised. I've told them a lot about our forefathers Abraham, Isaac and Jacob, and our family's history; and, of course, they've grown up with our Yiddish songs and they have a very close relationship with my mother and everything she represents.

R.O. What about your husband, is he Jewish?

J.R. No.

R.O. How does he deal with your Yiddish songs and your Yiddische Mama?

J.R. He himself is a theatre director, and he's always been very supportive of my commitments. He's never had any problems with my family – he's part of it, and he's always enjoyed the warmth of our *mischpoche*.

R.O. What about his parents?

J.R. They were both Communists. You see, the three great religions all have the same roots: they all worship father Abraham, Moses and Solomon. They all express the same idea, which is also present in Buddhism, and they all contain great humanistic ideals, and it is this humanistic message which links Judaism with socialism. But so far it is only socialism, or Communism, which has found a way to attempt to realize these ideals. Ernesto Cardenal once said: 'I am a Communist because I am a Christian.'

R.O. How did you come to be a Yiddish folksinger?

J.R. Every mother sings to her children, and naturally, I grew up with these Yiddish songs – Lin was always singing them when I was a young girl. I used to listen to her rehearsing just as my sons hear me rehearsing. Lin's *Yiddishkeit* implies a certain style that informed her life, and I grew up in that atmosphere too.

I became an actress and a singer, but it never occurred to me to sing Mama's Yiddish songs. I didn't live her life, I didn't have her temperament, and I would have found it embarrassing. Besides, children shouldn't just imitate their mothers. Then in 1979, when Anne Frank, had she lived, would have turned fifty, an evening was organized in her memory. My mother (who had met and become close to the Frank family in Westerbork and Bergen Belsen) was to sing and a friend of hers was going to read passages from the Diary. In the course of the preparations, however, my mother's friend who already had four children became pregnant again, and didn't feel well enough to continue: so Mama asked me to take over her part. I, of course, refused immediately, but then my family and friends said: 'This culture has to continue here, and who will represent it if not you.' So, at Mama's insistence, I agreed to do the programme with her. I reread the Diary, and I began to study Yiddish and Jewish history.

This evening for Anne Frank was produced as part of the (East) Berlin Cultural Festival in October 1979. Meanwhile, a few months before our 'evening', the film *Holocaust* was shown on television.[3] It was a very bad movie: that is, it emotionalized and commercialized the Holocaust without providing any historical analysis. It was a kind of Hollywood marketing of the Holocaust. But it had an enormous effect on people here, and it generated a great demand for our evening for Anne Frank which we also produced as a television programme and then as a record. This was a time of new discussions among a new generation of Germans: we all began to realize how dangerous the situation of the world is.

After this success, Lin and I did a concert of Jewish music – also sold out. Later my sister Kathinka joined us, with her fiddle, and I began to work with two guitarists. We started with Yiddish songs, but our new record, *Lid von Yontif*, also includes Hebrew songs and Sephardic romances.

R.O.   I know that your concerts are always sold out months ahead. What kind of an audience do you draw?

J.R.   Lots of young people, and also somewhat older: the age group that rarely comes, though, is the forty- to fifty-year-olds. But this age group includes many people who are under lots of pressure at work and have less time for concerts. Many of the young people may also be influenced by the resurgence of neo-Fascism, especially in West Germany, France, and the USA.

R.O.   Which songs do the people here like best?

J.R.   They like the happy Chassidic songs, but even those pieces are *zwischen schmejchl un trern* [between smiles and tears], because, you know, in Yiddish there is no song without some sadness in it. But there is also no song so sad that it doesn't contain an element of hope.

I remember I once gave a concert in Weimar in a hall not far from the former concentration camp Buchenwald: in fact the camp, located on the hill just behind the city, is a prominent feature of the landscape. It made me wonder how the people living in Weimar could not have known what was going on there, and why they didn't do anything about it. After the concert, an older woman in the audience stood up and said that in the early 1940s she was in her early twenties, and worked as a librarian. As she put it: 'It was clear to us that something strange was going on up there, but we were afraid to ask.' And she added that during those years she used to see an elegant young doctor come into the library regularly to borrow forbidden books, but it was only after 1945 that she realized that he was one of the doctors who had performed experiments on human beings. She said she just couldn't believe that such an educated man could be capable of that kind of systematic murder.

Another time a woman in her mid-fifties, who had been a child during the Fascist years, came up to me after a concert and, with tears in her eyes, she said: 'You know tonight I realized for the first time what an extremely rich culture the Nazis destroyed.' I told her that this culture was not destroyed and cannot be destroyed, though its form does change over time.

People often approach me after concerts with all kinds of questions about East European Jewish history, and especially how the survivors found the courage to go on living after what had happened. They also want to discuss the burden of guilt which the Germans brought on themselves. I think the idea of the guilt of a people is the wrong way to formulate the problem. There were also Fascists in other countries, and now there is a new Fascism. The central historical fact is rather the assembly-line murder or extermination that took place, and it was not only of one people because we shouldn't forget that Gypsies, homosexuals, Communists, and Social Democrats also perished in the camps. This was all part of a system, and the basic question is not one of the guilt or innocence of people, but of the necessity of understanding that kind of social order and precluding the possibility of its return.

R.O. I was very moved by your involvement with the Yiddish language and your commitment to making it live on. But the generation of Jews for whom Yiddish is the language of the struggle to create a better world is dying out. What do you see as the future of the Yiddish language and culture?

J.R. I've read, for example, in *Canadian Jewish Outlook*, that in North America there are Yiddish books, and even a Yiddish newspaper. And Lin and Eberhard told me after their trip to Canada that there's a broad movement – also cultural and reading groups – to preserve the language and bring it back to life. I think it's interesting that this attempt to rediscover one's origins or 'roots' began in highly developed, industrial countries like the US and Canada. I don't think you can really plan or programme this kind of thing. When the need is felt, for example, to get back in touch with Yiddish, to read it and speak it again, then it happens. I've heard that there are also Yiddish study groups in France. And I read the articles of Eva Brück (our correspondent in Birobidjan) and reports in *Sovietish Heimland* (Soviet Homeland)[4] which I get from Moscow, so I know that Yiddish lives and is still taught in Birobidjan and that Yiddish songs and literature continue to be written there. Language and literature always develop new forms, and I don't know how the language will sound in different parts of the world fifty years from now, but I keep hoping.

R.O. You talked about how the fiftieth anniversary of Anne Frank's birth motivated you to renew your relationship with your Yiddish background. Do you know of any other young Jews here who've had similar experiences?

J.R. There's never been very much of a Yiddish tradition in Berlin. Jewish tradition here was always a very assimilated one. It developed in German and Hebrew, but not in Yiddish. The East European Jews who immigrated to Berlin at the end of the last century were looked down on by the *Yeckes* (German Jews).

I once worked with a group of [non-Jewish] folksingers in Ilmenau[5] who were trying to learn some Yiddish songs. But they soon discovered that you can't just put the words and notes together and sing. These songs have two levels – at least two levels – of meaning: they're actually quite dialectical, and to sing them properly you have to understand the culture and experiences out of which they were written.

I know a few people here, Jews and also non-Jews, who are interested in Yiddish, but we don't have anything like a study or conversation group. That's really a problem for me. I can read, write, and understand Yiddish, but I can't speak it, and I have to read your newspapers to find out what's going on culturally; and every once in a while someone sends me a record from abroad. We really do need more communication and exchange with people in other countries.

R.O. I'd love to hear about your trip to Israel in 1983.

J.R. We went as a family – Lin, Eberhard, my sister Kathinka with her fiddle, and me, Jalda – at the invitation of the *Bet Hatfuzot* (House of the Diaspora) Museum in Tel Aviv. We stayed for four weeks, and during that time we gave ten concerts. We were incredibly warmly received in Israel, and the trip became a very deep and important experience for all four of us. For one thing, it became clear to us for the first time how interested the Israelis are in learning more abut the GDR and how it differs from West Germany. In Israel people know that there is another Germany, but that's all they know. While we were there we were dragged from one interview to the next till I thought I couldn't stand it any more. The five standard questions the Israelis asked us were:

1. Where did you get the names Jalda and Jaldati?

2. Are you allowed to give this kind of concert in the GDR?

3. Is there an audience for these songs in the GDR?

4. Are there any Jews left in the GDR?

and, of course:

5. How do you like our country?

Before we left for Israel people told us that Yiddish isn't spoken there any more so we should translate everything into English. And we thought about how we were going to introduce the different songs. But right after the first song, as we tried to speak a few words in English, people in the audience started to call out 'Nu? Red Mameloschen' and it became clear immediately that they all spoke Yiddish. Lin had known that kind of audience from her earlier years and from her trip to North America, but for me an *oylam*, a whole hall full of people who understand Yiddish and to whom I don't have to explain everything was a completely new experience and just fantastic!

The most moving concert we did was an evening for Anne Frank in Yad Vashem. Shortly before the concert began we had been in the Hall of Names, and we found the names of my mother's parents, grandparents, and the whole *mischpoche* that died in Auschwitz: we found out that my uncle Jakob died, not in January '45 as Lin had thought, but already in September '44. And in this building we gave our evening for Anne Frank. The hall was full of young people from all over the world, many between the ages of fifteen and twenty. We've never had such a fantastic, such a sensitive audience! They laughed and cried with us: they were with us every step of the way. We ended with Pablo Neruda's peace song, and I must say I felt that I had never before appreciated that song and the idea of peace as I did that night in Yad Vashem.

It was also very impressive and important for us to be able to explain a bit about the GDR in Israel and to describe Israel to our friends at home. People in the GDR really don't know enough about Israel, and I try to fill in some of the gaps. For example, very little is known here about the Peace Movement in Israel and how broad it is.

Another thing that struck me was how in Jerusalem Arabs, Jews, and Christians too, live together, accept each other as neighbours, speak each other's languages, and live a normal life together on a daily basis. I found this incredibly moving. I was also impressed by the green desert, the blossoming swamplands: how much effort was invested in this land and how fertile it is. You just plant what you will, throw a little water on it, and everything grows. There's enough land and water there for everyone. That Arabs and Israelis, as two peoples, can't have a normal life together there, as individual Israelis and Palestinians do from day to day, I found very painful. And I hope that one day they will be able to live peacefully together. That there's no peace there now we know is a result of the *divide et impera* (divide and rule) policies of the colonial powers. But, thank God, we met enough people there who want to end this war and to live in peace with their neighbours. We hope this will happen soon.

R.O. Has your trip to Israel had any effect on your work here?

J.R. Well, we're now expanding our repertoire to include not only Yiddish but also Hebrew songs; and we brought back a thick volume of Yemenite songs too. The Yemenite songs are just wonderful, but whether we, as central Europeans, can ever learn to perform them properly remains to be seen. I've also begun to study Hebrew. Hebrew is an important element in Yiddish culture, but I find it very difficult.

That was another thing that impressed me in Israel – the variety and richness of the cultural traditions that come together in that melting pot, and the way especially young people are working with them through all the media: cassettes, film, writing, etc.

R.O.   When you give a concert here, do people from the audience ever come up to you and engage you in a discussion about Israel, and do you feel that people in the GDR have prejudices about Israel?

J.R.   I wouldn't say prejudices but, rather, many people in the GDR have inhibitions about discussing Israel. They know very little about Israel beyond the cliché that Hitler exterminated the Jews here, and now the Jews are doing the same to the Palestinians in Palestine. It's always the photos of Sabra and Chatila juxtaposed with photos of Auschwitz and the implicit equation of the two. I feel very strongly that this equation is a false one, and whenever it comes up I try to explain to people a little bit about the history of the Zionist movement. I start with the increase in anti-Semitism that occurred in conjunction with the various national movements in all the industrialized countries at the end of the nineteenth century. I emphasize that Zionism was a reaction to anti-Semitism and that the first Zionist settlers in Palestine were people who had participated in the 1871 aborted coup against the Czar and then fled to Palestine to try to implement our ideals there. These original settlers got along very well with their Arab neighbours. The animosity developed only later as a result of the divide and rule policies of the British colonial government.

The present crisis in the Middle East and throughout the world should be seen as an opportunity – perhaps our last opportunity – to make this world a more humane one, to end the arms race and to use our material resources instead to feed the world's people. Only in this way can we prevent another Holocaust.

AUTUMN 1987

Lin Jaldati's and Eberhard Rebling's autobiography has been published: *Sag nie, du gehst den letzten Weg: Errinerungen* (Never Say that This is the Final Journey: Reminiscences) (Buchverlag Der Morgen, (East) Berlin, 1986). It ends in 1945. In this sense it resembles many autobiographies of heroes of the Resistance. Many younger East Berliners, and Westerners too, are eagerly waiting for the next volume, the personal and historical accounting or remembering of the twenty-five years from 1945 to 1970 – the post-war confusion, the Cold War, and the founding and establishment of the East German state.

Although Jalda Rebling still performs with her family, she now has her own group of three musicians who accompany her. And her interests and style have developed considerably over the last three years. Jalda Rebling was originally trained, not as a singer, but as an actress, and many of her current programmes include, in addition to songs, readings of poetry and prose which fill in the dimensions of the Jewish world she presents. Moreover, where Lin Jaldati's programmes – though varied – tend to emphasize the political struggle which organized much of her life, Jalda Rebling now sings Jewish songs that are more inward-looking and transcendent, even a bit religious. This contrast of two generations is quite common in East Berlin in the social and intellectual groups close to the Resistance and the Party.

Lin Jaldati died in September 1988.

Vincent von Wroblewsky

8 A Jewish Existentialist at the Academy of Sciences*
Dr Vincent von Wroblewsky

Vincent von Wroblewsky, a philosopher, was born in 1939 in Clermont-Ferrand, France. He earned his PhD in Philosophy in 1975 at the *Akademie der Wissenschaften* in East Berlin, where he has been a Research Associate since 1967. Von Wroblewsky has written many articles on French existentialism; his book, *Jean Paul Sartre: Theorie und Praxis eines Engagements* was published in 1977. He has two daughters, Rachel and Sarah.

R.O. I've heard that you're descended from a long line of European socialists. Are they the von Wroblewsky side of your family?

V. von W. The name Wroblewsky is known in the history of revolutionary struggles, going back to the time of the Commune. There was a Valery Wroblewsky, a Polish General who took part in the Polish military insurrection and then emigrated to France. There he became part of the military leadership of the Commune along with General Dombrowsky; and, after the defeat of the Commune, he fled to London where he functioned as the Polish representative and legal adviser in the First International. I'm not sure exactly how I'm descended from this Valery Wroblewsky, though it's quite certain that there is a connection. But it's also important to me and to my family that we've never researched our genealogy, that we never had to, and that we know very little about our distant ancestors. I once tried to find out a little more about it, but I heard that the archives in the town where my grandfather's family lived were destroyed during the Second World War, so that there are no documents from before then.

There are revolutionary traditions, socialist ones, coming from my grandparents too. My father's mother, for example, took part in the 1905 Socialist Congress in Amsterdam, and my mother too attended a Congress against War and Fascism there in 1932, just before the Fascists came to power here. I remember she told me that she attended as a representative of her Communist Party cell at Ullstein,[1] where she was working then.

---

*A shortened version of this interview was published in *Canadian Jewish Outlook*, September 1985.

My parents were both Communists since the thirties: that is, my father became a Communist in 1927, and my mother in 1931.

R.O.   Were both of your parents of Jewish descent?

V. von W.   Both of my mother's parents were Jewish, but my father had a Jewish mother and a non-Jewish father, so that, although three of my grandparents were Jewish, I bear the rather non-Jewish name 'von Wroblewsky'. My grandfather Wroblewsky married a woman from a family called 'Doktor'. My mother used to say that, with a name like that, her mother-in-law (with whom she had an ambivalent relationship) was an impostor from the moment of her birth. My mother's maiden name was Wohlgemuth and her family came from an area that is now part of Poland.

R.O.   Did your parents both identify as Jews?

V. von W.   Not my father, at least as far as I know. I don't remember my father: he died when I was four. He had emigrated to France where he fought in the Resistance. My mother grew up in Berlin, in the Jewish faith, in a Jewish orphanage called the Auerbach Institution. She was a half orphan, and the Auerbach Institution, which was funded by Berlin Jews like the Einsteins and the Liebermanns, enabled my mother to obtain a very good education which her own mother could not pay for. My mother came from a family of very modest means: my maternal grandmother was a seamstress for several of these wealthy Berlin Jewish families, the Einsteins among others.

R.O.   Did your mother have a traditional Jewish upbringing in this orphanage?

V. von W.   She had a Jewish upbringing; but when she was seventeen, she gave up the Jewish faith and became an atheist and a free-thinker. Then she met my father and with him she became a Communist. And in 1933 they emigrated to France.

My father first (and later my mother too) worked on the Dimitroff Committee in Paris,[2] and my mother also worked with Henri Barbusse on the Committee Against War and Fascism. Then, when Paris was occupied, my father was interned in a camp near Mans and my mother fled south to the unoccupied zone and stayed in Clermont-Ferrand, near Vichy. My older brother was born in Paris, I was born in Clermont-Ferrand, and my younger brother was born in Aubusson: that was their next stop, an even smaller town. It was in that area that my father was active in the Resistance. He died there in October 1944, at the age of forty, not in battle, but of heart and liver problems that were exacerbated by the years of persecution, illegality, and struggle. My mother returned to the GDR in 1950.

R.O. What made her decide to go back to Germany?

V. von W. ˛For her it was a political decision, like her decision to emigrate in 1933. My mother's family – her mother and brothers – had all been murdered by the Fascists. My parents had tried several times to persuade them to leave Germany. My mother explained to me that especially at the time of the 1937 World Fair in Paris she told her relatives that this was their last opportunity to leave. They said that they were saving money for tickets to Shanghai and would leave soon. Money was tight then and the Shanghai route was the least expensive. My mother's brother was awarded an Iron Cross for his military service in the First World War. My mother was the only member of her family who survived.

In 1950, in France, she met a German comrade she knew from before 1933. He told her about the founding of the GDR in 1949, saying: 'There's now a country where you belong. In France you've remained a stranger, though you've lived here for seventeen years'.

R.O. Did she have a job in France?

V. von W. Yes, but not work that challenged her interests and capabilities.

R.O. What kind of work did she do?

V. von W. All kinds of things. In the small village where we lived she took in sewing. In Paris she worked for a Jewish furrier and also did sewing. But here she's worked as a translator.

R.O. Coming from Paris to East Berlin as an eleven-year-old must have been quite a change for you.

V. von W. Yes, that was a rough one all right, but in post-war France we didn't know only prosperity and good times either. Once the war was over, my mother had to deal with the fact that she was alone with two children – my older brother had been killed in 1939 – living in a village of 800 inhabitants. Had she remained in Moutier-Rozeille (near Aubusson), her sons would have sooner or later had to go work for some local farmer. So her problem was to get out of the village and into a more promising environment. In 1946 we moved to Toulouse, and there she put us in a Jewish orphanage for three months. She worked as a seamstress for the orphanage so she could be near us.

The interesting thing about this orphanage was that its director was Golda Meir. Golda Meir was then in Toulouse organizing the smuggling of weapons into what was then Palestine, and preparing to transfer the children there too; most of them were Jewish orphans found in concentration camps and elsewhere. Naturally Golda Meir wanted to include the three of us in her plans, and she told my mother how proud she would be one day to carry an Israeli passport. But my mother, who

saw our stay in Toulouse as a preliminary phase of an eventual move to
Paris, held firm. She told Golda Meir: 'I'm not a Zionist, I'm a
Communist, and I don't want to go to Israel because it's not my home.'
Golda Meir then answered: 'I'm a Communist too! See, here's my closet,
take what you want, my clothes belong to everyone!' My mother said
that was Golda Meir's idea of Communism – sharing her clothes.

Anyway, in 1948 we moved to Paris, and in 1950 back to Berlin where
we would be able to get a good education. Although this probably seemed
quite natural to my mother because she was born and grew up in Berlin,
it didn't seem at all natural to me. And, of course, the Berlin she returned
to in 1950 was quite different from the city she left in 1933: the landscape
and the people had changed, and not necessarily for the better.

My memories of the move, as an eleven-year-old, don't necessarily
touch the essentials: they often dwell on the superficial details of life in
Berlin at the time. There were none of the Mediterranean fruits that we
took for granted in Paris, the shoe polish smelled awful, and I found the
way the children my age were dressed very odd. At that time they had
these shoes made out of very hard leather: they were called '*Bundschuhe*'.
And the girls wore sweatpants under their skirts when it was cold. Besides
which, when I came to Berlin I spoke no German.

R.O.   You mentioned that your mother worked for a Jewish furrier and
at the Jewish orphanage in France. When you returned to Germany were
her social contacts largely with other Jews in Berlin?

V. von W.   My mother had contact mostly with other returned emigrés,
both Jews and non-Jews. But whether or not they were Jewish was
incidental. They were emigrés who made a political decision to return to
the GDR. There were, naturally, many Jews among them, but they were
mostly Jewish Communists rather than humanistic Jews. As I grew older,
it became more and more interesting for me to listen to the stories of
their experiences during the years of their emigration. At that time my
mother lived with another woman (non-Jewish) whom she knew from
before 1933 and who returned to the GDR from England. She liked to
cook and invite people over, and the two of them spent a lot of time
with friends, all kinds of people, many of them actors and artists.

R.O.   Was your mother a member of the *Jüdische Gemeinde* at this
time?

V. von W.   No, she had nothing to do with the *Gemeinde*.

R.O.   Were the children you played with Jewish, or did Jewish children
have a special identity at that time?

V. von W.   That came to me only much later. Basically I experienced
something like a Jewish identity, or the problem of a Jewish identity only

after I came back to Germany. Through contact with other returned emigrés and through confrontation with German history, and the changes it brought generally and to my own family in particular – for me the big change of language and culture which the return entailed – my Jewishness became a problem and an awareness.

R.O. Did you experience any anti-Semitism at that time?

V. von W. I don't remember any.

R.O. Did your mother give you any kind of Jewish upbringing?

V. von W. She conveyed to me a Jewish identity only through telling me about her life: and she also used a lot of Jewish expressions in her speech. She wasn't religious, but she was very strongly Jewish.

R.O. So, for you being a Jewish eleven-year-old in Berlin in 1950 was quite comfortable?

V. von W. Well I've already told you about the material circumstances, and they weren't all that important. And, on the other hand, for many of the children my age, I was something of an exotic bird, and I attracted a lot of attention which was not unpleasant. And that compensated for some of the other problems. I mean during those early years I was in several different orphanages and that was not unproblematic. My mother was alone with the two of us. She had to work and she thought we would have a more orderly life there. But in my relations with the other children, being Jewish was never a problem.

R.O. Have you ever been a member of the *Jüdische Gemeinde*?

V. von W. No. I've gone to the synagogue a few times for the High Holidays, and I'm really interested in learning more about Jewish culture and history. For quite a while I've felt that it's something I've been missing and would like to catch up on. I'd really like to know more about the religion, the culture, the mythology. There are other things I miss too. For example, I never had the chance to learn to play a musical instrument. It bothers me a lot because I like music very much and would like to be able to make music too. It's something like my relationship to the Jewish background of my family that's also my background.

R.O. Is your wife Jewish?

V. von W. No.

R.O. But your daughter is named Sarah. How did you come to choose that name?

V. von W. Well, when we were expecting the baby, I very much wanted to give it a Jewish name, and I thought of Miriam for a daughter because

I like that name. Then, when my wife was in the hospital, she decided to name the baby Sarah. Maybe she wanted to go the whole way.[3] I don't know, but I agreed to it and it's a pretty name.

R.O. Does your wife give Sarah a Jewish upbringing?

V. von W. No she can't because she doesn't have the background for it.

R.O. How do you deal with your daughter's Jewishness?

V. von W. So far I have to say I haven't done anything. I've thought about it. It would be nice if there could be some kind of children's group in the *Jüdische Gemeinde* – and I believe there was once talk of forming one – where the children could learn some Jewish culture. I would gladly send Sarah. But I don't know how likely it is that they'll ever organize it.

R.O. Have you ever talked about this with anyone on the Board of Directors of the *Gemeinde*? After all, they do have a youth group for older kids.

V. von W. I think I once talked about it with Irene Runge. She said that they might be able to start something like that, but there are problems in the *Jüdische Gemeinde*: it's not a Reform congregation, but rather in many respects quite Orthodox.[4]

R.O. Are you a member of the Party?

V. von W. Yes.

R.O. Do you consider yourself an atheist?

V. von W. Yes.

R.O. Would that make it philosophically or personally difficult for you to be a member of the *Jüdische Gemeinde*?

V. von W. It depends on what's required. If being a member presupposes faith or belief in God, it would be difficult. But if it's a moral or cultural association, a special relationship, then fine.

R.O. Have you ever tried to join the *Jüdische Gemeinde*?

V. von W. No.

R.O. Did you ever think of joining?

V. von W. No. As I said, because I'm an atheist, I would never think of joining a religious community. That's a place for being religious.

R.O. Suppose there were a Jewish Community with perhaps a more secular or cultural orientation?

V. von W.   Yes, that would be more interesting to me.

R.O.   The *Jüdische Gemeinde* has cultural programmes once a month. Have you ever gone?

V. von W.   So far perhaps I haven't done enough in that direction. I hope I can change that. It's really like I said before about music. I have too much to do, many distractions and commitments, and there are some wishes and needs that are always getting pushed to the side.

R.O.   Are most of your good friends Jewish?

V. von W.   No, it's mixed. Jewishness is not the decisive criterion, but some of my good friends are Jewish.

R.O.   Since you moved to Berlin, have you ever returned to France to study or visit?

V. von W.   Until 1976 I went to France several times to do research and to participate in scholarly meetings. But since 1976 the French government has denied me an entrance visa and won't give me the reason. Some friends of mine who are French tried to find out why, and they learned only that there's a false denunciation against me, though I don't know from which side, so I can't defend myself. I hope that at some point this situation will change.

R.O.   Is there any kind of Jewish sub-culture within the Party in the GDR, among people like you, for example, who feel Jewish but have no relation to the *Gemeinde*?

V. von W.   I wouldn't say so. There are many individuals who fit that description but there's no group dynamic among them.

R.O.   Do any Israelis – Israeli students at Humboldt University perhaps – ever surface in the Party?

V. von W.   I didn't know that there are Israeli students at Humboldt. I guess those kinds of things you hear of via Canada.

R.O.   Is there a particular Jewish sensitivity to certain policies of the Party, for example, its Middle East policy?

V. von W.   I couldn't say.

R.O.   Is there any contact between Jews in the Party here, and the Israeli Communist Party?

V. von W.   There is contact, I believe, but not at the grass roots level. When I was younger, especially during the years when I was a student, I frequently worked as a translator at Congresses here. I translated at several Congresses of the *Fédération Internationale de la Résistance*, and there I became sensitized to the problem of the many political groups within Israel and the role of Israeli representatives in international organizations, and their conflicts with Arab representatives. But at the grass roots level very little is known about Israel and there are no direct ties.

R.O.   Do you personally have any contact with Israel through relatives or through your travels?

V. von W.   No.

R.O.   What would you add to the description you've given of Jewish life here?

V. von W.   Jewish life here isn't limited to what Jews articulate and non-Jews mediate. There are also several non-Jews who, as a result of the course of German history, take an interest in Jewish history and have made some valuable contributions. I'm thinking especially of Heinz Knobloch's book about the role of the Mendelssohn family in Berlin.[5] People like Knobloch take great pains to ensure that a tradition, a memory that became endangered through the Holocaust that took place here won't be lost. One can't easily separate or compartmentalize Jewish life here precisely because there are people like this: and I'm not talking about the unpleasant kind of 'philosemitism', though I've experienced that too.

R.O.   What do you see in the future for Jewishness in the GDR?

V. von W.   It's a difficult question. It's a tragedy that I find very painful, even though I'm not religious. The *Jüdische Gemeinde* here is so small and there isn't even a Rabbi. It really is threatened with extinction as a result of the Fascist heritage. I hope that it doesn't become extinct, that it will survive and develop further. I also hope that everything that Jewish culture was will remain in the public consciousness through literature and art where there is much but there could be still more.

R.O.   Have you ever dealt with your Jewish identity or with any Jewish themes in your scholarly work?

V. von W.   Only indirectly. My work on Sartre was interesting especially as it related to my own existential experience and being. Existentialist philosophy is a framework for the expression of one's own identity: to what extent it is necessary or incidental and to what extent it is predetermined or the result of one's own decision. When I consider the possibilities of my own life, there's much that's accidental, the weak spots, in Spinoza's words, the *determinatio est negatio*, that excludes another possibility. For example, my mother explained to me that when she was young she was engaged to a Jewish doctor who was a Zionist and wanted to go to America. She ultimately broke off the relationship because her political commitments were so different. That would be the first place where it could have gone otherwise. It wouldn't have been me biologically because the father would have been different, but I could have just as easily been born and grown up in America. Or in 1946, if my mother had gone to Israel with Golda Meir and the other children, then I might be living in Israel today. Perhaps I would have never learned German and would have only a very distant idea of Germany as the land of my ancestors. And so there are many points which lead one to question what one's own identity depends on, and to what extent one is the creator of one's identity.

For this reason Sartre's thesis that man makes himself or is what he makes himself is important for my own experience. And I think that through this history, also through this Jewish history, it is different for me than, I believe, for someone who is born in a small town, grows up, has a family, and dies there as his family has done for generations. That has a different character of determination and the particularism is more self-explanatory. By contrast, for me, this possibility and also what I've absorbed – for example I think in French which is my mother tongue, I read more French than German, and I have essentially Jewish ancestors. These are diverse elements, not necessarily free of contradictions, to be melted into a unity. But I believe that these internal tensions, the cultural contradictions within one, can also be something productive. Identity, then, shouldn't be understood simply as identity, but as what has been lived out, in the more Hegelian sense as dialectical identity. And I believe that there, also in this sense, one finds perhaps a generalized Jewish experience in the larger history of man, that does not accidentally necessitate, for example, that dialectical thought derives to a large extent from Jewish thought.

AUTUMN 1987

Vincent von Wroblewsky was one of the fifty names on Irene Runge's list of East Berliners who might be interested in establishing contact with the Jewish community (see p. 52), and he has been an active member of the new group since its first meeting. In early December 1987, at one of the group's meetings, he presented a paper on Sartre's concept of anti-Semitism. He was invited to lecture at the Hebrew University in Jerusalem in December 1988.

Clara Berliner

9 Returning to Berlin from the Soviet Union*
Clara Berliner

Clara Berliner† was born in Berlin in 1915. She emigrated to Paris in 1933, to Moscow in 1935, and she moved to the German Democratic Republic in 1956. Ms Berliner received a degree in nursing in 1940, but after her return to Germany, she worked for the state news services.

C.B. I am a Marxist and a Communist, and therefore I don't have much to do with religion. Moreover I come from a very assimilated family. In contrast to those Jews who immigrated to Berlin from Russia and Poland after the First World War my family had a rather loose and Liberal Jewish awareness. We went to Temple on the High Holidays, my younger brother had a Bar-Mitzva, and some of our friends were married in the synagogue on the Fasanenstrasse,[1] but that was the extent of our relationship to Judaism, even in my parents' and grandparents' generation. But we knew that we were Jewish.

I attended a girls' *gymnasium* in the West End of Charlottenburg, at Reichskanzlerplatz: Jewish girls constituted 26% of the student body there. The few who came from recently-immigrated Jewish families did not have an easy time. There was a social distance. But in the middle classes one perceived little anti-Semitism before 1933.

R.O. You describe yourself as Marxist, or Communist. Were your parents Communists too?

C.B. No, God forbid!

R.O. So how did you become one?

C.B. It was a sign of the times. In those days millions of Germans were unemployed, and young people who were politically interested had to draw their own conclusions and take a stand. I took the Communist route: I was influenced by friends, and also, as I mentioned, by the social conditions – the absolute hopelessness. One saw the dangers of Fascism, but, at the same time, with a certain blindness, one thought that perhaps

---

*A shortened version of this interview appeared in *Outlook*, September–October 1987.
†A pseudonym.

it might come out differently. There was a strong Social Democratic Party and there was a strong Communist Party, but the working-class parties were not united and were therefore unable to prevent the Facists from taking power.

R.O.   How old were you when you became a Communist?

C.B.   Seventeen.

R.O.   And were you the only one from your middle-class *gymnasium* to join the Communist Party, or were you one of many there who made that decision?

C.B.   In the Communist Youth Group in the West End of Charlottenburg there were a lot of working-class boys – it was mostly boys, few girls – and a few came from intellectual families, but I don't see social background as being that important. Marx and Lenin didn't come from working-class families, and in my generation Anna Seghers, Stefan Hermlin, and Peter Edel[2] all came from the middle class, so I wouldn't say that I'm an exception.

R.O.   Did your becoming a Communist cause any conflicts in your family?

C.B.   My parents didn't take the whole thing very seriously until April '33 when the police saw me distributing leaflets and came to search the house for illegal literature. That October I moved out of my parents' house and went to live with a friend – a wonderful woman who later became a sculptress.

R.O.   How did your parents take all this?

C.B.   They still weren't concerned. I was still quite young, it happened in the best families (as they said), and they really didn't believe that the consequences would prove so far-reaching over the long term. And, I should add, as children we had a very liberal upbringing. When my parents finally began to appreciate the seriousness of my commitments and their implications, they were naturally shocked, but they were also very nice. Without my mother's help I would never have obtained a visa to enter France. She managed to arrange the visa through friends and acquaintances at a time when crowds of people stood in line at the French Consulate every day for hours, only to be turned away.

After I left Germany in 1933, I did political work in Paris: and I had very little money. In Paris I met my husband: he was a construction engineer from Berlin and a Jew. In 1935 he took a job in Moscow. That was an important move for us.

We lived in Moscow from 1935 to 1956. At first I worked as a translator, synchronizing the translation of foreign language films into Russian: it was horribly tedious and boring. Later I became a foreign language teacher: I taught German and English. Actually before I left Germany I had wanted to study German literature. When that became impossible I thought of becoming a doctor, so I didn't regret it too much when I ultimately became a nurse in Moscow.

R.O. Why then did you decide to return to Germany?

C.B. It was actually my husband's decision: he was ten years older than I, and also better educated. Our families had both emigrated to London, and our parents were getting on in years and wanted to have more contact with us. But in spite of all this, I can tell you quite honestly, it was not an easy move for a German Jew, and I found it quite difficult. Don't forget I had been living in the Soviet Union for twenty years and I was very well integrated there

R.O. So it was your husband who decided to move back to Berlin?

C.B. Well, it was really the whole family. My oldest son was in his early twenties, and there were educational opportunities for him in the German Democratic Republic. My younger son, though, was still a little boy – he was only two-and-a-half years old.

R.O. How did your older son take the move to Germany?

C.B. It was actually quite interesting and also a bit complicated. In the Soviet Union he had been living in a Communist student residence where everything, down to the potatoes and onions belonged to the group. When he came here and saw that each student had his own potatoes and his own onions, he found it infuriating, but he soon got used to it.

R.O. You've said that you have a strong Jewish awareness, but that you're not a member of the Jewish Community here. Could you elaborate on that a little?

C.B. I'm not a member of the *Gemeinde*, but I attend all of their cultural events, and Dr Kirchner and I have worked together for years on the Committee of Anti-Fascist Resistance Fighters. When I returned to Berlin in 1956, one of the first things I did was to go to the Jewish cemetery in Weissensee to find out what had happened to our family graves: my maternal grandparents had bought a plot, my husband's father was buried there, and my great grandparents too. I was quite surprised that all these graves were still there, and I immediately took over the responsibility for their maintenance. At this time my husband was quite ill – he died soon after of heart disease – and I arranged for him to be buried in Weissensee with his family. I feel strongly that, wherever one stands politically, one should know where one comes from, and with which tradition one's family is associated. That's a very important part of cultural history, and I've tried to communicate that idea to my sons. My mother does not share this opinion, nor does my sister who has become a staunch Anglican. But I feel that after Auschwitz one is obligated to take one's origins, one's past, seriously.

R.O.   So after you came back to Germany to further your husband's career and your son's education, what did *you* do?

C.B.   Well, you know, it wasn't really a career decision. We're Germans, we're fourth-generation Berliners, and we're Communists. In 1949 the German Democratic Republic was founded, and the GDR took great pains to enable those who had fled the Nazis to return. We talked about it as a family, and decided to move back, though I have to say, it was not an easy decision.

It's probably difficult for you Canadians to imagine how much was done here for the anti-Fascist resistance fighters. In a city that was all but destroyed, we were given a three-room flat with warm water and central heating in a beautiful old building. It was fabulous! My older son was immediately accepted at the university, though he didn't speak a word of German, and my little boy, Sascha, got a place in a kindergarten.

R.L.   Did Sascha adjust to Berlin easily?

C.B.   My Sascha has wonderful red hair and that made him very attractive and a bit exotic. That he spoke only Russian was not a problem because that was the language of our allies and friends. Sascha was very popular in the kindergarten. One day he did come home and ask why he was called Sascha and not Hans, but he realized that it was in no way a problem.

But I really don't want to minimize this move: it was not at all easy. I was over forty, and my husband was over fifty and had lost his entire family except for his parents and his brother – they all perished in Auschwitz. One naturally looked at everyone passing in the street and wondered what they were doing from 1933 to 1945. We knew that *theoretically* in the GDR the past had been overcome, but it was quite a while before one really felt integrated and at home.

R.O.   How did Sascha understand and react to what you were experiencing?

C.B.   Here what happened in Germany under the Fascists is discussed thoroughly in the schools and not only at home. And it is considered a great privilege for a child to be the son of a resistance fighter. You orient everything around the Jewish element. I can understand that that's the theme you're working with, but we don't make those distinctions. I'm first and foremost an anti-Fascist: to see our struggles as merely Jewish experiences would be to deny the importance of the Christians in the

Resistance without whose help many Jews would never have been able to escape.

R.O. I can appreciate the importance of the schools' assuming the responsibility for educating children about the Fascist period. But there's a difference between abstract knowledge, or what one learns in school, and direct confrontation. I've read and thought quite a bit about the Nazi times in Germany, but when I moved into a furnished apartment in Zehlendorf in 1982 and found swastikas stamped on the bottom of the dinner plates, I almost fell through the floor.

C.B. We really shouldn't have any illusions on that score. Even the Kohl government has had to acknowledge how strong the neo-Nazis have become in West Germany, especially since the Christian Democrats have come to power. I don't want to sound like some kind of agitator, nor do I want to play down our problems and conflicts, but you have to understand that here *we're* the victors and *we* have the power.

Just for example, think of all the American Jewish literature that's been translated and published in the GDR – Saul Bellow, Malamud, Singer, and I think even Philip Roth. For intellectuals this is incredibly important. And have you heard of our artist and illustrator Anatoli Kaplan? My son Sascha has an original of one of his graphics. It makes me really proud, but unfortunately I can't find anyone to frame it.

R.O. So you feel, then, that Sascha hasn't really been affected by all you've been through.

C.B. No, not at all. You have to understand that when we moved here he was still very young. These are also very private feelings and, quite honestly, as a citizen of this country, one has to be a bit restrained. When Sascha was six he began to go to school in Prenzlauer Berg, the neighbourhood we lived in, and I joined and became active in the Parents Association and the National Front.[3] I was used to this kind of activity because in Moscow I had been one of the leaders of the nurses union in the hospital where I worked. These kinds of organizations play a large role in our society, and they were important in my reintegration here. As a member of the Committee of Anti-Fascist Resistance Fighters I regularly visit schools in my neighbourhood and explain to the children what happened in the Soviet Union during the Second World War: how women and children lived there, and how difficult the victory was – things that I know from my own experiences.

For the last ten years I've been involved in a project with the Commission for the Study of the History of the Resistance. We're interested in the history of our neighbourhood, and I often go with children from grades 7 and 8 (or alone) to the older comrades – we call them *Arbeiterveteranen* (worker veterans) – and we ask them about their lives and experiences during the twelve years of Fascism and how they survived. We've heard lots of incredibly interesting stories, and we're now writing it up as a pamphlet. The schools in the GDR have many activities that are organized from the top down. I think it's important that projects are also initiated at the grass roots level. We now have a Workgroup of Young Historians. Every year the children organize an exhibition. These are very important and impressionable years in a person's life, and a responsible adult (either a history teacher or a parent) is needed to guide the children in drawing up and carrying out their plans. But this is living history.

R.O.   These kinds of projects have been tried in many West German schools. The experience there is that the going tends to get rough when the children go home and discover that at least some members of their own families, and often the teachers too, are former Nazis.

C.B.   That doesn't happen here. For one thing, here it is absolutely impossible that a young person with those tendencies would ever be allowed to become a teacher. Occasionally you do hear a parent or a grandparent using an expression like (when it's too noisy) '*hier geht's ja zu wie in der Judenschule*' (it sounds like a Jew school in here). I don't feel that that's discrimination: we've always had expressions like that in Germany, but one still shouldn't say it here. When I was a child in Charlottenburg, there was a game called *Der Jude hat ein Schwein geschlachtet* (the Jew killed a pig), but we never thought of it as anti-Semitic.

So long as my husband was alive I had no contact with Jewish life here. I had enough work just getting settled: my husband was very ill, and Sascha too was often sick. My husband was no more religious than I, but when he died, I had him buried at Weissensee. He would have turned over in his grave if he knew that Cantor Nachama[4] sang prayers over his shrouded body, but I found it the right thing to do and I'm not afraid to say it out loud. I later grew closer to the *Jüdische Gemeinde* through my contact with Dr Kirchner. I'm really proud of the way the city of Berlin has reconstructed the synagogue on the Rykestrasse, and the *Gemeinde* organizes such beautiful concerts and interesting lectures. As a Communist, of course, I have my own ideas about Israel, but one shouldn't confuse anti-Zionism with anti-Semitism.

R.O.   Have you ever been to Israel?

C.B.   No, but several of my husband's relatives live there, and I read Leberecht's[5] reports from Tel Aviv. I'm turning seventy this year, and I don't want to paint things too rosy, but I think your readers should know that for us the problem is solved. As an anti-Fascist resistance fighter one has a social and political status in the German Democratic Republic that you can only dream of in other countries.

AUTUMN 1987

In September 1987 Clara Berliner's son Sascha joined the Jewish Community. Sascha is also an active member of Irene Runge's group.

Alfred Katzenstein

10 Jews, Germans and Psychotherapy in the German Democratic Republic

Dr Alfred Katzenstein

Dr Alfred Katzenstein was born in 1915 in Mönchen-Gladbach, Germany. In 1933 he emigrated to France; then to Holland, Spain, and the USA. He received a PhD in Clinical Psychology from Kansas University (USA) in 1952, and settled in the German Democratic Republic in 1954. From 1954 to 1958 he worked at the Bezirkskrankenhaus für Psychiatrie und Neurologie, Brandenburg. Since 1958 he has been associated with the Institut für Herz- und Kreislaufregulationsforschung der Akademie der Wissenschaften der DDR. In 1963 he received his Habilitation at Friederich Schiller University, Jena, and was named Professor in 1970. In addition to his clinical work and research, Dr Katzenstein served for many years as President of the Gesellschaft für ärztliche Psychotherapie der DDR (GDR Society for Medical Psychotherapy). He has written many articles, and his book, *Psychotherapie: Wege zur Veränderung von Einstellung und Verhalten* (Akademie-Verlag, Berlin, GDR), was published in 1980. This interview benefited from the unexpected but welcome participation of Alfred Katzenstein's wife, Dr Ursula P. Katzenstein.

As a scientific personality Freud commands the respect and sympathy even of those who are critical of his work. He is one of those who, despite many attacks and disappointments, steadfastly stood for a basic idea which was essentially justified in the context of the times: namely the idea that certain human diseases and sufferings have psychological causes and can be neither understood nor treated without reference to the person as subject. (A. Katzenstein and A. Thom, 'Die Historische Leistung und die Grenzen des Werkes von Sigmund Freud (1856 – 1939)', in Alfred Katzenstein, Helmut Späte, and Achim Thom (eds) *Die historische Stellung und die gegenwärtige Funktion der von Sigmund Freud begründeten Psychoanalyse im Prozess der Formierung einer wissenschaftlich fundierten Psychotherapie* (Bezirkskrankenhaus für Psychiatrie und Neurologie, Bernberg, GDR, 1981) p. 21, interviewer's translation.)

A.K. I was born and grew up in Mönchen-Gladbach; it was a small German city near the border with Holland, and my family was pretty well known there. My parents were very Liberal Jews; we went to synagogue on the High Holidays and – rarely – on other occasions. My mother once had an angry confrontation with the Rabbi. He tried to stop me from going to my violin lesson one Saturday morning: he felt I should go to synagogue with him instead. I no longer liked playing the violin and would have been at least as happy in synagogue, but my mother prevailed. So I belonged to the Jewish Community – sort of – until my Confirmation, my Bar-Mitzva. After that I became more and more sceptical, questioning things, but without any definite idea in mind yet.

Before 1933 there was relatively little anti-Semitism in my class at *gymnasium*. There were about twenty-five students in the class; four of the boys were Jewish. About half of the class was organized in the *Jugendbewegung*, the *bourgeois* youth groups. It was quite a large movement, mainly of young people who were against the false pretences of the older generation. We went on long hikes and lived close to nature on weekends and during vacations. Similar groups existed in various shades; thus there were Social Democratic as well as nationalistic groups. Groups of Catholic, Protestant and Jewish religious denominations, and some others.

The three Jewish youth organizations were Habonim, Hashomer Hazair, and the group I was in, the Kameraden. In 1932 the Kameraden split into three groupings. The Naumann faction was very German nationalist and pro-Nazi even though it was Jewish; there was a Zionist faction that later settled in Israel, mainly in Kfar Szold; and there was a socialist group. I felt some sympathy for the Zionist and socialist tendencies. Some of the other boys in my group were socialists, but my father was a capitalist, so I thought socialism was something for workers and not for me. I first bcame acquainted with socialism when the Soviet film, *Weg ins Leben* by Makarenkov, was shown in Mönchen-Gladbach. I went to see the movie mainly because my girlfriend had threatened to see it with another boy if I didn't go, but the film made a deep impression and influenced me greatly.

Then in 1933, I was confronted quite directly with Fascism. I was attacked on the street a few times – they called me 'dirty Jew' and so forth and ran after me. And the SA began to assemble for their marches on Staufenstrasse, right in front of our house. I had known the leader of the Communist Youth Movement in Mönchen-Gladbach casually. One day after Hitler had become Chancellor, I met him on the street and he complained that many former members no longer participated in group activities. 'They're all afraid.' I was seventeen or eighteen at the time, and that challenged my courage, so I assured him that he could count on me.

In June '33 my girlfriend and I went to Amsterdam for the week-long Pentecost holiday; vacationing in Germany had become too dangerous, and her sister was already living in Amsterdam. While I was there I read all the literature I could find on the *Reichstagsbrand*. I was so impressed that I felt this had to be known among my acquaintances too, so I took some of this material home, typed and duplicated it, and gave it to a few friends. A few days later the Gestapo came and arrested me. At this time I had hardly any political understanding, and I was certainly not prepared to be put in prison under the terrifying circumstances which then prevailed. Fortunately the Gestapo officers who arrested me were older men – in the beginning the Nazis took over all the old staff. These two men, one of whom had once been a Social Democrat were – fortunately – interested in making money. My father was willing and able to pay, and so I was eventually released after a couple of weeks under great strain and uncertainty in jail. My parents took me over the border to France – visas had not yet become a problem – and sent me to a great-uncle in Calais.

I didn't stay in Calais for too long. On the pretext that I had to get my visa renewed or something, I soon left for Paris. I had obtained some addresses there by writing to *L'Humanité*,[1] and in this way I came into contact with the anti-Fascist *immigration*. I had no work permit at this time, but I worked illegally as an auto mechanic.

My stay in France was ended forcefully in 1934. On 12 February the French Fascists held a large demonstration to terrorize the Chamber of Deputies. Two days later the Communists and Socialists called for a counter-demonstration. I didn't want to go, but a friend of mine suggested that we just watch from a distance. And suddenly we were in the middle of it all at the Place de la Bastille. When a detective tried to arrest my friend, I intervened – since my friend did not speak French – and so we both spent that night in jail along with twenty or so other foreigners. We were mistreated considerably that night and, when the press was brought in, the reporters were told that we were the international troublemakers who started the demonstration. The next day two agents took us to the Belgian border, instructed us where to cross to avoid the border patrol, and assured us that, should we return to France, they would deport us to Germany.

From Belgium I went on to Holland and, through a friend in our anti-Fascist group, I found a young pacifist who agreed to take me on as an apprentice radio technician. I lived with him for a year in Roermond, a small city right across the border from Mönchen-Gladbach, and I got back in touch with my German comrades and my family. I also got back in the business of organizing outings with the friends who visited me in Roermond, and incidentally used the occasion as an opportunity to distribute anti-Fascist reading material. Then one day our group was infiltrated and one of our German comrades was arrested. We found out who the informer was, took his passport and wrote in it 'Police Agent' so that he couldn't tell any lies about us to the Gestapo. When his superiors saw what we had done, they complained to the Dutch authorities that we had mistreated a German employee (which was not true) and mishandled his passport (which was correct). So I had to leave the border region.

I had no place to go but Amsterdam and, since I had no job there and no place to stay, on the advice of some Jewish people in Roermond, I went to the Jewish Refugee Committee in Amsterdam. They told me point blank that they had no way of helping me unless I joined the Zionist Movement. I told them that they'd have to convince me first, as I considered myself a socialist. The woman interviewing me was impressed by my honesty and agreed to take me on probation. So from 1935 to 1937 I lived in Amsterdam in the *Beit Hehalutz*, the group home for the Zionist Pioneers; I even became a leader of Hehalutz. I never became a Zionist, but some of the Zionists became sympathetic to Communist ideas.

Meanwhile the Spanish Civil War had begun, and one of our Communist comrades had gone to Spain to fight in the Republican Army. That Christmas we had a very emotional meeting in the home of a Dutch intellectual. There was a Dutch piano player, some German actresses who recited poems, and then the wife of this comrade read his letter from the front. I felt that this was a point where I had to prove that my conviction was not just talk, so I volunteered for Spain. I then had four very anxious months: I feared the Spanish people would win the war without me. But then, one morning, I got a telegram to report to a particular place and soon I was on my way to Spain.

From 1937 to 1939 I fought as a *Voluntario de la libertad* in the 11th International Brigade of the Republican Army. In February '39 we crossed the border to France to lay down our arms, and we were interned in French concentration camps. I was in various camps from 1939 to 1941, when my family, who were now safely in New York, arranged for my visa and passage to the United States.

Earlier my father had been quite prosperous, and he felt that Nazism was not so bad. The bad thing was his son who was a Communist and who got the whole family in trouble. When he was arrested in 1938 during *Kristallnacht*, and jailed for ten days, he found out that Nazism was bad. As soon as he came out of jail, he went to the American Consulate in Koblenz and looked up 'Katzenstein' in the New York telephone directory; there were about two pages of Katzensteins and he wrote to all of them. Eventually one of these Katzensteins – who was not a relative – agreed to sponsor the immigration of my sister and brother, and when I arrived in New York in October '41, the whole family was there, even my grandmother.

For the first couple of months I worked with my brother at a diamond tool factory on Chambers Street. But after Pearl Harbor in December '41 my brother was inducted into the army and, by the end of '42, I was too. When I had completed basic training at Fort Meade, I was sent to Memphis to (I think it was) the Fourth Army, the so-called Home Army; there I read and excerpted sixteen newspapers every day for the general of G2, the head of intelligence. After three months of this they sent me to intelligence training school – A. P. Hill – and from there to counter-intelligence.

So when I returned to Germany I was a CIC Special Agent with the US Army Ninth Infantry Division. My job was to find potential and actual saboteurs who might impede the progress of our unit. We were one of the first units to cross the Siegfried Line, but later we were encircled by the German counter-offensive at the Ardenne Bulge, and we were cut off again by the Germans at the Remagen Bridgehead. I had the great luck of being able to arrest the *Gauleiter* of Munich, thanks to my good contact with the anti-Fascists who had survived.

After the war I returned to New York and, at the suggestion of my wife and friends, I enrolled at New York University under the GI Bill. Still impressed by the Makarenkov film, I thought of becoming an educator. A degree in education would also be useful when I'd return to Germany – we had always planned to go back. But when I registered at NYU, it was already late in February and the only opening was in social work, so I took it. I was very disappointed with social work because I felt this was just how to do well and with what means you can do a little better, but it was not really analysing the source of people's problems. So after receiving my BS, I went to study clinical psychology at Kansas University. KU had a special programme for mature students which combined the regular PhD studies with clinical training, and this appealed to me.

R.O. Why did you decide to study in Kansas rather than return to study in Europe?

A.K. At that time there was no way for me to go back to Europe. As an American I could go to Europe only as a member of the US Army.

U.K. In the United States we got a stipend under the GI Bill of Rights. Had we returned here, we would not have been Americans any more, and whether they would have let us study here was another question. At that time you couldn't just come here and say: 'I want to study.' That was the last thing that Alfred's friends told us: 'Study and finish because here you can learn something.' And there aren't many Communists here who came back to Germany with a university education. Those who returned came from concentration camps, from prisons, and from hiding: very few were university educated.

A.K. At KU I trained in psychoanalytic therapy. My tutor was Dr Modlin, a practising psychoanalyst. But what I did was psychoanalytically-oriented therapy: it's shorter than psychoanalysis and it doesn't utilize, for example, free association and dream analysis. Instead there's more emphasis on character analysis and interaction.

I wrote my thesis on three methods of psychotherapy with schizophrenic patients: one was a psychoanalytically-oriented individual therapy, one a psychoanalytically-oriented group therapy, and the third was a social process-centred group therapy. This is the sort of therapy that I have continued to develop since then, a therapy that emphasizes social involvement and social process rather than focusing primarily upon the development of the isolated individual in the therapist's office.

I got together a group of eighteen chronic schizophrenic patients from the wards who had no perspective of ever leaving the hospital. One of these patients, for instance, had previously been tentatively discharged and had gone to the mayor's office and asked for Adolf Hitler; so, of course, he came right back. I had chosen the task of trying to raise the level of confidence of these patients so that they would be able to leave the protective milieu of the hospital. We employed these three methods in three parallel groups. With the individual psychoanalytic therapy group the analyst (Dr Kamersley) talked with the patients individually about their specific problems with the goal of making them see their way to a more independent existence. In group therapy I attempted to achieve the same goal in a psychoanalytically-oriented group setting.

Now in the social process-centred therapy we brought the patients together and proposed that as a group they should design a project to prepare themselves to leave the hospital in three months. One patient came up with the idea of writing and performing a play: 'We could play the story of our lives.' Somebody else said: 'But I would never be able to go on the stage.' A third member of the group then proposed: 'Well, maybe we could do it with puppets.' Slowly the idea evolved of doing a puppet show, and since some patients felt they couldn't even talk on the stage, they decided to record the dialogue, so that members of the group would only have to move the puppets. And in the group discussions they came up with some marvellous ideas.

The play was, of course, about a patient who is discharged from the hospital. He comes home and asks his father for the car keys. The father answers: 'No, once crazy, always crazy, I won't give you the keys.' Then he goes to his former employer, and the employer says: 'Oh, wonderful that you're back,where have you been? Oh in that hospital, well then you'd better come back next week. We don't know whether we have an opening for you.' Everybody rejects him except his girlfriend: she stays with him. But then he's very disappointed and he goes to a place where the water is deep, and he looks down and the Devil is behind him and says: 'It's wonderful there. You just jump and everything will be all right – all this trouble, employers, parents, will be gone for good.' But just then his best friend comes along and saves him; and he, his friend, and his girlfriend start a new life.

The patients wrote this play, they built the puppets themselves and learned to move them, and then they built the stage. First we performed the play in the hospital, and then someone came up to us and said: 'We have to play it for the employers association.' And so we did this too, and it was a big success. Most important, of the six patients in the group, five left the hospital.

R.O. So your thesis, then, demonstrates that the social process-centred therapy is the best of the three considered?

A.K. No, I don't say it's the best: our sample is too small for that. I say it's at least as good as the other two for this particular purpose. For other purposes it may not be as good, and in some cases it may be even better, but that still has to be demonstrated.

R.O. Was it conflictful for you to work at an institution like the Menninger Clinic and to be a member of the Communist Party?

A.K. No, I didn't see it as conflictful. We were fifteen trainees in one year at KU. It was very stressful training: in the first year, five of the fifteen ended up in the hospital as patients. We were of all political orientations. My colleagues knew that I had strong socialist convictions; whether or not I was a Communist was not so important.

U.K. We were always members of the German Communist Party in emigration, but we were not members of the American Communist Party. This is a very important distinction, because if we had been members of the American Communist Party, it wouldn't have been as easy as it was for us to return. You see, at that time you needed the permission of that Party, and the American Communist Party was never very strong, and they didn't like to see people go. This is very understandable, but we never became members of the American Communist Party, though we had close contact with many people who were members.

R.O. Was there a relationship at this time between your political beliefs and your work with your patients?

U.K. We've always tried to integrate our Marxist ideology into our work. If you just take the way this therapy was conceived, you can easily see that it is not oriented around a strong egocentric idea, but it is seen as a social process. In order to make the patient well, you have to make him understand what is going on socially, and you have to make him find his way through this society.

A.K.   We left the US in October 1953, we stayed in Holland for six months, and we reached Germany in May 1954.

R.O.   What was it like to come back to Germany as a Jew after the Holocaust?

A.K.   There were many unknown factors, and we really didn't know what to expect, but we knew that we belong here. When we left the US I reckoned with the possibility that I might be jailed for up to a year while they checked my identity and background. That didn't happen. We didn't expect to be greeted with open arms because we might have been agents, but still there were a few times when we were quite taken aback. My first job here was at the hospital in Brandenburg. After I had worked there for two years, one of the doctors confided to us: 'You know at first we all thought you must be either drug addicts or criminals. Why else would you come over here?'

U.K.   It was a bad time here. In America you can go into a store and buy whatever you please. When we came here, you could get food only with ration cards, and even then the items for which you had coupons weren't always in stock. We didn't expect it to be much better, but to adjust to that was still quite difficult.

A.K.   What shocked me sometimes was the fact that people don't trust each other as much as I had hoped in a socialist society. In 1958 we came to Berlin: in the early years here there were times when impertinent remarks I had made as jokes were utterly misunderstood and reported by colleagues to the director of the hospital.

U.K.   We always had good relationships with the authorities, with friends, with the comrades on the Central Committee, and with those with whom we were together in emigration. But the professionals and intellectuals with whom we worked were always suspicious of us. In the early 1950s there was bad propaganda here against America. Of course there are lots of things one can say against the United States. But what was said was so primitive and so terrible, and people who didn't know otherwise were, of course, influenced by it.

R.O.   Can you explain a little bit about psychotherapy in the GDR?

A.K.   We have a society for psychotherapy: it's called the Association for Medical Psychotherapy, and there are approximately 1500 members (about 250 in Berlin), but not all psychotherapists are members of the group. The most prominent schools are behaviourist psychotherapy, psychoanalytically-oriented therapy, and the Rogerian type which we call *Gesprächstherapie*.

R.O. Is there a Jewish presence in the psychotherapeutic profession here?

A.K. No, in fact at the moment I can't think of any other Jewish psychotherapist in Berlin.

R.O. Are you a member of the Jewish Community here?

A.K. No. Since my Bar-Mitzva, I've visited a synagogue once – in Budapest, to look at it. During my years in Amsterdam I read a lot about the history of the Jewish people, and now I read Kemelman[2] with great interest.

R.O. You mean *Friday the Rabbi Slept Late*?

U.K. Isn't it wonderful!

R.O. When did your children become aware of their Jewish background?

A.K. I think they were about seventeen or eighteen when they realized they were Jewish. It never played any special role for us.

R.O. How did they react?

A.K. They took it casually. Actually later on my younger daughter had a friend who took her to a synagogue, and then they wanted to know a little more. But there are so many things that they don't know about our lives.

R.O. Have your daughters ever experienced any anti-Semitism here?

A.K. I know that among older people there is still anti-Semitism, that's clear. My older daughter's friends were quite frank. They told her: 'You know my father said he never dreamt that his son would go out with a Jewish girl.' But still my daughter and *her* friends could discuss this in a relaxed and natural way.

R.O. Are you still working?

A.K. I see patients part-time, and I supervise some PhD theses.

R.O. Do you still do group projects like the one you wrote up in your thesis?

A.K. No, I don't do that any more, but I still tend to focus on the social life of the patient rather than exclusively on his individual development, though in this business one also has to be a little flexible.

R.O. What kinds of problems do your patients have?

A.K.   I have patients with cancer, patients with severe marital problems, others with sexual inhibitions – a bit of everything.

R.O.   Are many of your patients Jewish?

A.K.   Lately, yes, but I think that's because one hears from the other.

R.O.   Among your Jewish patients do you find any kind of Jewish syndrome or emigré-child syndrome?

A.K.   One has to be very careful with such labels. I think marginal groups always have difficulties adjusting. All those who go from one country to another, and those who return to their own country have adjustment problems. What is decisive is the extent to which the parents are able to master their conflicts without getting the children too greatly involved.

R.O.   Could you be a little more specific about the kinds of things that come up?

A.K.   Well, let's talk about the convinced Communists. When they returned from emigration they unavoidably faced conflicts between their Utopian theoretical conceptions (even if they are not Utopian but scientific socialists) and the reality which they face here. These conflicts can be very painful, and sometimes people bitch. Adults understand that there is a solid socialist conviction underneath the angry words, but children do not. They hear and react to the expressed anger and pain..

   Also some of the emigrés who returned retained their families' foreign citizenship which entitled them and their children to special privileges: they could travel where other people couldn't, etc., and this contributed to the conflicts their children had to deal with.

R.O.   When Jews of the post-war generation come to you for psychotherapy, to what extent is their Jewishness part of the problem?

A.K.   Let me give you an analogy. We know that in certain heart and circulatory conditions smoking and obesity are risk factors. But when you have a patient with heart and circulatory problems, the fact that he smokes and is overweight doesn't really mean very much. You have to ask why does he smoke, and why is he overweight? And then you start looking at problems which lie much deeper. In the same way when you say Jewishness is a problem for some emigré children, yes, that may be a problem, but the central conflict may go much deeper.

R.O.   Are you suggesting, then, that Jewishness is often a mode of articulating another kind of *malaise*?

A.K.   Yes, exactly.

R.O. Have you ever thought about whether Jews have a special place in GDR society, or whether GDR society affects Jews in a unique way?

A.K. No, I haven't thought of it in that way. I have played with the idea of eventually writing an autobiography, and there certainly the Jewish problem would come up. But it's not a problem to the extent that you may think it is. I'm not talking about Poland or the Soviet Union, but in the German Democratic Republic we are very well integrated, and I don't think it's a problem.

Ursula Katzenstein (left) with Robin Ostow

11 From Germany to the German Democratic Republic via Palestine, France and the USA

Dr Ursula Katzenstein

Dr Ursula Katzenstein was born in Berlin in 1916. She attended the West End School in Charlottenburg until 1933 when she had to leave because of her political activities. She then learned cabinet-making, first in Palestine, then in Berlin and Paris at the École Professionelle de l'Ameublement. In New York, Dr Katzenstein studied occupational therapy for four years at New York University School of Education. In 1954 Dr Katzenstein settled in the German Democratic Republic; there she worked at the Brandenburg-Görden Hospital for Neurology and Psychiatry, and initiated the programme for occupational therapy there. Since 1958 Dr Katzenstein has been living in (East) Berlin and has been employed at the Klinikum Berlin-Buch where she founded the programme for occupational therapy for the physically disabled and the programme for the education of occupational therapists; this programme has been incorporated into the curriculum of several schools for paramedical workers throughout the GDR. Dr Katzenstein has been active for many years in the GDR Society for Rehabilitation. In 1970 she earned her MD at Humboldt University. Dr Katzenstein currently works part-time as Director of the Department of Research and Documentation at the Klinikum Berlin-Buch Rehabilitation Centre. This interview benefited from the unexpected but welcome participation of Ursula Katzenstein's husband Dr Alfred Katzenstein.

U.K. All these problems and troubles and questions about Jewishness: I would hate it. I lived in Palestine for four years after I left Germany, and all these questions never occurred to me at all.

R.O. So then why did you go to Palestine?

U.K. Because I had to, where else should I go? I was seventeen, and my father had to send me out of the country for political reasons. I was a member of the Communist *Jugendverband* (Youth Federation), and I was involved in many things, and somebody told my father that pretty soon something would happen, and he had to send me out. He said: 'You are a seventeen-year-old girl, I can't send you to Paris alone. I can't support you; I don't have the money.' But the Zionists sent out girls' groups, and children's groups, the *Jugendaliyah*. So he signed me up and I went to Palestine, but not because I wanted to.

R.O. What did you do in Palestine for four years?

U.K. I joined the Communist Party. It was completely illegal. First I was in a girls' school for agriculture. Then I was sick, and I never went there again. I was living with a boyfriend in Tel Aviv and I learned cabinet-making. Then I was interned because in 1936 the Arab people in Palestine started a general strike against the Jewish underground, against the taking away of work by the Jewish workers. As soon as the Arab landlords sold their land to Jewish organizations, the Jews wanted Jews to work on the land, and the Arabs became unemployed; they became landless. In '36 the situation was so bad that the Palestinian Arabs began a general strike. The Palestine Communist Party was Arab and Jewish; it was the only party which had members from both nationalities.

As Jewish Communists, we supported this general strike of the Arab people which was the national liberation movement on the Arab side. We were arrested and put in prison. The prisons were all in Arab towns, in Jaffa, Haifa, and Jerusalem. Arab lawyers defended us because the Jewish lawyers were forbidden by the lawyers' association to defend Jewish Communists. The Arab law association gave us one lawyer in each town who defended only Communists without our having to pay. While I was in prison I learned Hebrew; before, I didn't have the time. I spoke more or less Jewish; it wasn't really Jewish, it was broken German. Jewish is really an old-fashioned German, from the Midde Ages. But when you speak German, you learn Jewish much more quickly than Hebrew.

I was in Jaffa in prison, I was in Haifa, and I was in Bethlehem, in the women's prison. And from there they wanted to deport me to Germany, the *Jews*. The Jewish police department tried to deport me to Germany. My friend had just been released from prison and he arranged that, instead of going to Germany via Italy, I got a transit visa via France.

A.K. He arranged to pay some of the guards if they would let her go on this French ship.

U.K. Yes, but we also had to bribe them at the French Consulate for a visa. We went from Haifa on a French boat to Marseilles, without money, without anything. Then we went to Paris, where we lived from 1937 to '39. In Paris we had to make a living somehow. We couldn't get work permits: emigrants didn't get permission to work in France. So I went to work as a maid for some time. I was an excellent maid, though I hate nothing more than doing household chores. And then I started my own cabinet-making shop. I rented a garage, and pretty soon I had four boys working for me. I made a very good living, up to '39.

In '39 the World War broke out. On 30 August 1939, the French mobilized their army, and they arrested German anti-Fascists, but not systematically. We were arrested, and put in prison in Paris; and six weeks later, we were put into concentration camps. There was one concentration camp for women, and I became an inhabitant there. A friend who had gone to the United States earlier, a very good friend of mine, Professor Bergmann – he was an assistant of Professor Einstein's and is now the head of the Einstein Society – he did everything to get an affadavit for me and for my boyfriend. And by '41 we succeeded in getting a visa for America, and we went to the United States in September 1941.

R.O. You must have been relieved. Is that when you started to study occupational therapy?

U.K. Not quite, not right away, because first of all we didn't know English very well. We went with the Bergmanns to Black Mountain College, near Ashville, North Carolina. A new college was being built and we went there: the Bergmanns as teachers, and we were there with our friends. The college agreed to give us housing and food for three months. We would help them build houses, and after three months we went to New York. I started studying occupational therapy after America entered the war, because then the Jewish organizations had money also for women. Before, they only had money for men to study. But when the men went into the army I could get some of the money for university tuition. I studied at the school of education at NYU.

R.O. You said you were in the German Communist Party. What were they doing in New York at that time?

U.K. Well the young people formed a group of Nature Friends. While my husband was in the army I studied, and after he came back, we moved to Brooklyn. Our oldest daughter went to a day-care centre in Brooklyn. Then in 1948 we left for Kansas.

A.K. You know my wife was a Girl Scout leader there.

U.K. We lived in a very small town, and when people wanted to be nice, they said: 'Well, you see, we are Methodists, why don't you join the Methodist Church?' I said: 'No, because we are Jewish.' They said: 'Why not, why can't you come to the Methodist Church when you are Jewish?' I said: 'Because I don't go to church at all.' And they were very nice with us. And so, of course, our older daughter Katie became a

Brownie, and later a Girl Scout. But I didn't want them to learn what those people wanted them to learn. I thought the Brownie laws are very good: if I become a Brownie leader, I can interpret them differently. You see that is also somewhat political work.

I gave great speeches on international friendship. There was International Friendship Week and I was invited to talk at the school my daughter went to. The hall was filled with children, and I started out by asking them: 'What do you want for Christmas?' And they said ball, bicycle, this and that. And I said: 'What do you think the Russian children want for Christmas?' And it was quiet, and then one said: 'Maybe also a ball? Maybe also a bicycle?' So we came to the point where they found out that the people in the world want the same things that they want. And apparently the principal of the school and the teachers liked that, because I was invited to every school in the area. My little daughter didn't like to sit while I was talking in front, so I set her behind me on the stage and she held on to one of my legs. But that was a kind of political education one could attempt.

R.O.   Your children were born in North America then. Does that mean that they are US citizens?

U.K.   Well, every child born in America remains an American citizen all his or her life, so our daughters are also American citizens.

R.O.   Have they ever gone back to the US?

A.K.   No. They don't want to. They are GDR citizens.

U.K.   We decided that you can't stay here with one leg and stay there with the other leg. It isn't good for your own personality. Therefore, when we came here, we became GDR citizens, and our children too, and they were educated here and never knew as children that they could ever be American, and we found that they developed very well.

R.O.   How old were they when they came to the GDR?

U.K.   One was eleven, and the other five.

R.O.   How did they take the adjustment?

A.K.   Well, it was a little difficult for the older one: she cried when I told her: 'We are here now.'

U.K.   'And we're staying here.'

A.K.   We were a little afraid the last days before we came here because we had some very bad experiences, you know. Not only the Rosenberg case, but there had also been a case of Russian emigrants who wanted to return to the Soviet Union: their children were taken away from them before they could board the ship.

R.O.   By the Americans?

A.K.   By the Americans.

R.O.   Just for spite?

U.K.   No. A Communist is not allowed to educate American-born citizens.

R.O.   In other words, 'you can go but your children belong to us'.

A.K.   Exactly. That's what they said at that time. This was during the McCarthy period. And so we were afraid. When we arrived in Frankfurt, before we came over to Berlin, we were afraid something might still happen: somebody might take the children away from us. And so when we finally arrived in East Berlin, I said, 'Now we are there!' And the older one asked: 'What do you mean?' And I said: 'Now we are behind the Iron Curtain!' And she started crying because she had learned in school that all the bad people are behind the Iron Curtain.

U.K.   Wasn't much different from what Reagan says now. When I heard you talking to Alfred before, I realized that you lived in a different America than we did. When you started living, our America ended. Our experiences in America ended in '54: that's about when you started growing up and becoming conscious of your surroundings. Therefore we have to explain to you a little more than to older people, because the McCarthy period was only a slight little bit worse than what Reagan does now. In a way it's worse now, but in terms of internal politics it was worse then. Our daughter had learned in school that the Russians would throw atom bombs at us, 'and you will have to sit under the benches, so you will be protected from the atom bombs'. And so they rehearsed in class getting under the bench quickly, the silly things. They also had a school newspaper that was completely anti-Soviet.

R.O.   Which school was this?

U.K.   This was in Topeka and in Lawrence, Kansas; in all those schools.

R.O.   Since you've returned to the GDR have you given your children any kind of Jewish education or upbringing?

U.K.   We are not practicing Jews. We didn't give our children a Jewish upbringing.

R.O.   Do they take any interest in their Jewishness?

U.K.   Yes, they take an interest in it because that's 'in' right now, you know. If you are anywhere a little bit Jewish, it's very fashionable to play that up, because there aren't many of that kind left any more. And our children are interested in learning something, a little bit about Jewish history, and so on.

A.K.   But not very serious.

R.O.   You said it's currently fashionable to be Jewish. How does this get expressed?

U.K.   By becoming members of the Jewish *Gemeinde* (Community), by reading the books that come here.

A.K.   Our children are not members of the Jewish Community.

U.K.   No, our children are not members, but the Jewish *Gemeinde* makes concerts and this and that, and they go. Giving the children a Jewish education didn't conform with our ideas. And if we would have educated them in the Jewish way, it would have been terrible, because they couldn't have ever found a Jewish husband here.

R.O.   Is either of them married?

U.K.   Both are married, and we have seven grandchildren.

R.O.   And are both husbands non-Jewish?

U.K.   Yes, of course.

R.O.   Does that ever become a problem?

U.K.   No. One of our daughters has got a divorce, but not because of her being Jewish or something. And the other husband is the son of an anti-Fascist resistance fighter, also a member of the International Brigade, like Alfred is. Alfred and the father knew each other already in Spain. This was a much older man: he's dead now. But one day he said to Alfred: 'Well, you know, my son needs a wife; he needs a girlfriend, and I like your daughters very much.'

It was funny because my younger daughter was at that time eighteen or so. At first she said: 'I don't want to have a husband by your choice.' But finally she said: 'Well, why don't we invite them.' We knew the parents; she knew the parents too, and we were all members of the Socialist Unity Party. So we invited them; we were always very close to them, but the children didn't know each other because the boy had been in Rostock in the army for three years. They came; the father sat here, and the mother sat there, and the son sat there, and we sat on this side of the coffee table. It was just like in the old Jewish families with the *schadchen* (matchmaker). And it worked. Next time you come to Berlin call us up and come over because you really should meet our children.

AUTUMN 1987

Ursula Katzenstein told me that her older daughter Kate is a member and a regular participant at meetings of the group of East Berliners whom Irene Runge brought into contact with the Jewish Community (see p. 52). Ursula Katzenstein herself never attends programmes at the *Jüdische Gemeinde*, but she has come to accept Kate's decision and to appreciate the importance for every individual of exploring and coming to terms with the many facets of his or her identity.

III
Two Interviews Conducted in West Berlin

Thomas Eckert, with a portrait of his grandfather, Hermann Budzislowsky

12 The View from West Berlin*

Thomas Eckert

Thomas Eckert, born in 1953 in East Berlin, is a third-generation socialist Jewish journalist. His maternal grandfather Hermann Budzislawski (1901 –78) was the founder and, after 1934, Editor-in-Chief of *Die neue Weltbühne*, a well-known left liberal journal in pre-war Germany. In exile in the United States during the 1940s, he worked as a ghostwriter for Dorothy Thompson. After the war he returned to the German Democratic Republic and was appointed Director of the Institute of Journalism at the University of Leipzig. Budzislawski's daughter, Beate Eckert, worked for many years with the East German television, radio and news agency. Thomas Eckert, her son, was a journalist in East Berlin. He is currently writing a PhD dissertation in Political Science at the Salomon Ludwig Steinheim Institute for German Jewish History.

T.E.   All four of my grandparents were Jewish. I know almost nothing about my father's parents. My mother, though, comes from an old Jewish family in Berlin. My great-grandfather was a kosher butcher: he had a shop in what is now Käthe Kollwitzstrasse in East Berlin. His wife helped him in the store; she died a natural death in Berlin in 1936. My great-grandfather stayed in Berlin until 1938, and then, at the age of seventy, emigrated with my grandparents and my mother: first to Czechoslovakia; then to France; then, in 1940, crossing the Pyrenees on foot, to Spain, Portugal, and finally the United States. Imagine a seventy-year-old walking across the Pyrenees! My mother was then fourteen or fifteen years old.

My grandfather's Jewish identity was actually quite complicated. He was no Orthodox Jew. He was religious in his youth, and later moved to the left and became a Communist. To be a religious Jew and a Communist isn't easy. But even as a Marxist and Communist, he was sentimentally Jewish. One example is the High Holidays. My grandfather never knew exactly on which date they fell, but he knew they begin in September, so every year at the end of August or the beginning of September he would start asking 'When are the Holidays?' Once he

---

*This interview was originally published in *New German Critique*, Spring–Summer 1986.

knew, he didn't go to synagogue, but he thought about the Holidays at home, ate kosher food on the Holidays, and fasted on Yom Kippur. For him, being Jewish was no longer a *Weltanschauung*, but a culture. He was aware of his Jewishness and of the Jewish traditions, though he didn't give me a Jewish upbringing.

R.O. Are you talking about your father or your grandfather?

T.E. My grandfather. I grew up in my grandparents' house. My grandparents and my mother returned to the GDR from the United States in 1949. Like many other emigrés who returned, they had a very difficult relation to Germany. It was hard to go back there knowing that part of the family had been murdered. Though the political climate bore the promise of better times to come, the emotional relationship was nonetheless strained. My grandparents never resolved these problems, they just repressed them. My mother still hasn't worked out her emotional relation to Germany. Perhaps because Nazism and emigration were childhood experiences for her, they were that much more emotional and traumatic, and less amenable to rational or political analysis.

R.O. Are most of her social contacts with other Jews?

T.E. There are very few Jews in the GDR, that is, very few who still own up to being Jewish. After the war many people stopped letting on that they were Jewish. You can see that in the small size of the *Jüdische Gemeinde*. But in the last couple of years that's been changing.

R.O. Tell me more about your mother.

T.E. My mother studied history at Humboldt University. Then she worked for twelve or thirteen years with the East German television station. She later worked with the East German radio and with the news service. She now has a pension.

R.O. And your father?

T.E. He died two years ago. After the war he studied German literature. He then worked for many years in various Party functions and later held a research position at Humboldt University. He was also one of those Jews who never worked through their experiences of Nazism, and repressed everything that happened before 1945.

R.O. Are you an only child?

T.E. No. I have two sisters. One is a doctor: she's a year younger than I am. And the other one just entered university. I think she's studying Philosophy or Sociology, but I'm not sure, because I have very little contact with them.

R.O. How is it that you grew up in your grandparents' house?

T.E. Well, my grandparents saw that my mother was having a hard time emotionally and still hadn't come to terms with living in Germany. This is particularly complicated in the GDR in the sense that *theoretically*, because the socialist state overcame Nazism and capitalism, it is everyone's 'home': everyone can identify with the state completely and unconditionally, and, because the socialist relations of production have done away with exploitation, theoretically everything is all right. *Practically*, however, people do feel distanced from the system, but they are also under pressure to conform and to identify with the state. My mother never resolved this contradiction. She was constantly torn and dissatisfied, and she found it extremely difficult to raise children in an environment in which she herself felt so profoundly uncomfortable. My grandparents observed all this and offered to take care of me, so I moved in with them. Since that time I've become more and more distanced from my mother, to the point where I now have no relation with her at all. I know that she lives in East Berlin, and I might also find her address, but that's about all.

My mother's problems in psychologically readjusting to Germany are common among returned emigrés of her generation. My grandfather once described to me my mother's first impressions when they returned from America. My mother knew about Germany – that is, Nazi Germany – mostly from newsreels and from the stories she heard from my grandparents and their friends. The newsreels particularly tended to feature these huge, horrible Nazi parades: kilometres of Germans carrying torches and chanting '*Führer befiehl–wir folgen Dir*' ('Command, Fuhrer, and we'll obey you') and all that. My mother came back to Germany in 1948 and saw again these huge parades. The political content was different: this time it was the FDJ, the Communists, the SED, etc. But for her the visual image of large parades remained associated with Nazi Germany, and she asked my grandfather, 'What's going on? I thought those times were all over!' For her the continuity of certain forms confused the clear political changes that had taken place.

Many of the emigrés who returned to the GDR had a hard time readjusting, and some never made it. Recently several writers, some of whom are Jewish, have left the GDR: Günther Kunert, Jurek Becker, and earlier, Carola Bloch (the widow of Ernst Bloch) among others. If you ask them why, there are always many reasons. The real emotional reasons are incredibly complicated, perhaps even too complex for an outsider to understand.

R.O. You said that when you were a child there were very few Jews in the GDR, but that the situation is changing. Could you say more about that?

T.E. The Jewish emigrés who came back to the GDR were, for the most part, Jews and Communists, both together. They came to the GDR as Communists to build a socialist Germany in the Soviet-occupied Zone. Their Jewishness they regarded as incidental. Those who were Zionists went off to Palestine, though there were also some who returned to the GDR from Palestine. The writer Arnold Zweig, for example, though whether he was actually a Communist is a difficult question.

At any rate most of the Jewish emigrés who returned kept their distance from the *Jüdische Gemeinde*. For one thing, in the early post-war period the Jewish Community was, to many, suspect, because during the Nazi years the Board of Directors never destroyed the membership files. These files are now in the GDR State Archives in Potsdam. This is a very serious charge because without access to the Jewish Community membership files, the Nazis would have found it much more difficult to round up and deport Berlin Jews. And, in fact employees of the *Jüdische Gemeinde* not only turned over their membership lists to the Gestapo, they even helped draw up the lists of individuals to be deported, and helped organize the deportations. Individual Jewish functionaries collaborated in these ways in the hope that, in return, they and their families would be spared. This behaviour, of course, gave the Jewish Community a bad name.

Because of its troubled history, people often make the mistake of seeing the *Jüdische Gemeinde* as not only a religious group, but also as a political home for its members. And this discussion is always coming up in the GDR. When someone asks you about your (or your parents') relation to the *Jüdische Gemeinde*, there is usually the implication that Jews ought to be involved with the Jewish Community. But that's not always true. Right after the war, especially, many Jews kept their distance from the *Gemeinde*, though one must add that, before the deportations, many Jews in Berlin were incredibly naïve. They believed that because they had served in the German army in the First World War and, in many instances, were decorated for outstanding service, nothing too bad would happen to them. At that time it was still unthinkable that an entire race would be exterminated. Political people who read *Mein Kampf*, which was published in 1924, knew what Hitler had in store for them, but more naïve types saw it merely as some kind of propaganda.

If you ask me how things have changed, the *Jüdische Gemeinde's* cooperation with the Nazis can't be reversed; nor has it been forgotten; but the policy of the *Jüdische Gemeinde* has changed. The Jewish Community in the GDR has identified with the post-war reconstruction and the realization of socialism in the GDR; it is in no way in opposition to the state. And in the GDR the *Jüdische Gemeinde* is recognized, respected and generously financed by the state. You can see that the *Gemeinde's* less than two hundred members are in no position to maintain its two large cemeteries, and the old age home, to say nothing of the reconstruction of the synagogue on the Rykestrasse. Right now many of the children of Jews who resettled in the GDR are beginning to work through and discuss their past and their Jewish identity, very much the way they do in West Germany. But in the GDR when young people start to think about what it actually means to be Jewish, they don't necessarily look to the *Jüdische Gemeinde* for the answer.

R.O. Does this recent interest in Jewish identity in the GDR have anything to do with generational conflict? Is it perhaps a rebellion against the militant atheism of the older generation of Communists?

T.E. I don't see this as a generational conflict. In fact I have the feeling that the parents and grandparents are actually glad that the children want to have some relation to Jewish culture. Besides which, some members of the *Jüdische Gemeinde* in the GDR are also members of the SED: the Party and the *Gemeinde* are no longer mutually exclusive. These days going to religious services at the *Jüdische Gemeinde* in no way implies opposition to the state.

R.O. Can you tell me a little bit about your Jewish identity?

T.E. Well, actually I'm not a real Jew, because, for example, I'm not circumcised. No one ever raised that as an issue until I came to West Berlin. Here they're telling me to have it done, and I will have it done some time. There must have been someone to do circumcisions in East Berlin at the time I was born, but my family didn't arrange to have it done, and I can live with that.

R.O. Tell me about your childhood.

T.E. My childhood was relatively uncomplicated.

R.O. What kind of Jewish upbringing did you have?

T.E. None.

R.O. Were most of your friends Jewish?

T.E. In the GDR there are no special schools or classes for Jewish children. I grew up mostly with non-Jewish children. That is, I'm sure some of my friends were Jewish, but who was Jewish and who wasn't played no role in our relationships, and most of my friends probably didn't know that I'm Jewish. It certainly wasn't important to me at the time.

R.O. When did you first hear about the Nazis and the death camps?

T.E. I remember one awful incident. I don't know whether this was my first encounter with the Nazi period, but it made the most lasting impression. I had no Bar-Mitzva, but in the GDR we have a kind of secular confirmation: it's called *Jugendweihe*. When you're fourteen years old, you pledge your support to the state and to socialism in a public ceremony, and you're recognized as an adult. In preparation for the *Jugendweihe* there is a series of meetings, sort of like confirmation classes among the Protestants. Our classes were a kind of preparation for citizenship. We learned some of the history of our country, we went on excursions to the theatre and to the observatory, etc. One of these trips was a visit to the former concentration camp at Sachsenhausen. Our guide explained to us exactly what the Nazis did to the Russians, Poles, Jews, Communists, and Social Democrats there, and we were shown the instruments of torture and death. While I was there I picked up a flyer with information about the camp, and I brought it home with me. That evening when my mother saw the flyer, she fell into a fit of rage, and beat me up. I was totally perplexed. It was only much later that I came to understand that people whose relatives perished in the camps can't handle that kind of confrontation.

I should add that, although this was the first time I had to deal emotionally with the Nazi war crimes, in the GDR Nazism and the atrocities committed then are discussed thoroughly in the schools, so our visit to the former concentration camp was not to learn something new, but rather to confront what was known at a new level. For me, to stand at such a spot, and then to come home and to learn in such a violent and personal way that my own relatives died that way came as quite a shock.

My grandfather's brother, Herbert Budzislawski, was a member of the Herbert Baum group in Berlin. This was the only Jewish resistance group operating within Nazi Germany. In May 1942, they set fire to a Nazi exhibit called *The Soviet Paradise*. This exhibit about life in the Soviet Union was meant to convince the German population that Russians are an inferior race. The group was exposed by an informer, and all but two members of the group were executed at Plötzensee in Berlin. The Weissensee Jewish cemetery in East Berlin has a monument to the twenty-seven members of the Herbert Baum Group (including my great-uncle) who were executed, most of them in their early twenties. Herbert Budzislawski was the most well known, but certainly not the only member of my family to be murdered by the Nazis, to say nothing of the families of my mother's friends. For us, Jewishness, or a Jewish awareness, is perhaps first and foremost an emotional relation to the Nazi past. Everyone knew that six million Jews were killed, but a number like that, or any number is so impersonal. This kind of personal and emotional encounter with Nazism that I experienced at age fourteen (and, by the way, I don't hold it against my mother that she beat me) first touched many other Germans in 1979 when the film *Holocaust* was shown on television.

R.O.   How did you find your way to the *Jüdische Gemeinde*?

T.E.   As far back as I can remember I knew that there was a *Jüdische Gemeinde* in East Berlin, and I had passed the synagogue quite frequently. But to outsiders the *Jüdische Gemeinde* in East Berlin looks like a community behind closed doors. To become part of it is complicated, incredibly complicated. Sometimes you get the feeling that it's a frozen conspiratorial brotherhood because it has so few members and they all joined when they were young and have known each other for decades. For me, joining was a completely pragmatic step. When, in 1982, I applied for an exit visa from the GDR, I immediately lost my job and was barred from working as a journalist. I looked around for a new job and the only position I found was with the *Jüdische Gemeinde*. I worked there for a year, part of the time at the Jewish cemetery in the Schönhauserallee.

R.O.   Did working there strengthen your emotional relationship to your Jewishness or change your life in any other way?

T.E.   'Emotional' is the key word in your question. Actually I have a somewhat unusual relationship to this cemetery where I worked. It is located in what is now called Käthe Kollwitzstrasse, the street in which my great-grandfather had his kosher meat store. Although for years the cemetery was closed to the public, my grandfather once took me there: he had discovered that the small side door was usually open. Together in this deserted cemetery which hadn't been cared for in years, we looked at the graves of many people my grandfather had known personally, as well as at the graves of important Jews in the community. As we were leaving, I looked up at him, and was moved watching that man who must have been seventy years old, confront the graves of friends and relatives he had buried there. Jewish identity does have something to do with the cemetery. You stand there and look at the family histories inscribed on the gravestones and find parallels in your own family history. And you know which families knew each other and that your family belonged to that community too.

Ten years later when I worked at this cemetery, I began to research my family's history and the history of the Jews in Germany, and I noticed the connections. In this way something very practical, a job I had to take, led me to an intimacy with my Jewishness and my past that I hadn't even known I was missing. In that sense I don't regret at all the year I spent working there.

You know before this experience, a lot of my identity had to do with things I couldn't understand about my parents' and grandparents' behaviour and subjects one couldn't raise with them. This was the first glimpse I got of what my family's identity and past actually looked like. Although much of it isn't pretty, it isn't the worst identity either. Most

Germans have to worry about what crimes their parents may have committed during the Nazi times and are now repressing. It's comforting for a Jew to be able to know that his family had nothing to do with all that. It's very hard for me to imagine how a German can identify with this country. And many Germans are rightfully reproached for identifying without thinking about their past. It really should be made clear to the Germans what they've actually done.

R.O.   This brings me to another question. Have you ever experienced anti-Semitism in East or West Germany?

T.E.   I've never experienced anti-Semitism in West Berlin, but I've only lived here for five months. In the GDR there is anti-Semitism, but it's not publicized the way it is here. In the year that I worked at the Jewish cemetery in East Berlin I occasionally found gravestones that had been vandalized, and in Buckow, an area where I used to live, on the outskirts of East Berlin, there is a well organized neo-Nazi group. It has about ten or fifteen members, mostly adolescents who identify with Nazism, run around the place with their hands raised, shouting 'Sieg Heil!' and glorify the achievements of the Nazis. And, strangely enough, nobody does anything about them. It would be easy to say that this is just adventurousness or some kind of opposition to the state. I see it as people who can't cope with their past. I should add, though, that this kind of activity is in no way encouraged by the state. I don't know very much about this group's activities or motives, but they're still around.

R.O.   Tell me a little about the *Jüdische Gemeinde* in East Berlin.

T.E.   Well, as I mentioned before, it's very small, and it gives the appearance of being some kind of sect or lodge. The *Jüdische Gemeinde* does not sponsor cultural events for the public. It merely tries to maintain Jewish tradition through religious observance. As an organization it is just about impenetrable to outsiders. If you don't understand the Jewish customs and rites, no one there will bother to explain them to you or to introduce you to Jewish life. Either you understand it all or you don't. For example, these days there's just about no way to learn Hebrew in the GDR, and how much can you learn about Judaism when you can't read Hebrew? To become a member of the *Jüdische Gemeinde* there is so complicated that you often get the impression that they actually don't want to let people in. They talk a lot about getting new members and they complain that they are such a small group, but when you go to services there, and look at the faces around you, you feel like you're staring at a wall. If there are ten or twelve people there, they look you up and down like, 'Who is he? And what's he doing here?' So it really takes a bit of courage to go back a second or third time and a lot more courage to try to join. I wonder how long the *Gemeinde* can survive with this kind of attitude and behaviour. In fact many of its members' children have not been absorbed into the Community.

R.O. If it's so difficult for an outsider to be accepted at the *Jüdische Gemeinde*, how did they come to accept you and offer you a job?

T.E. Well, on my part, it was an act of desperation because I couldn't find a job anywhere else, and it just happened that my lawyer is also the lawyer for the *Jüdische Gemeinde*, so he helped arrange it. I have to add that hiring me was a bit risky for the *Gemeinde* – as it would be risky for any religious organization in the GDR, Protestant, Catholic, Jewish, or whatever – because there's always the possibility that if you hire someone who's applied for an exit visa, you might become identified with the exit visa and with its unpleasant associations. In the GDR it's not really proper to hire those kinds of people. So, for this, I'm very grateful to the *Gemeinde*; it's very much to their credit that they helped me so graciously. The fact that I come from a respected family may also have something to do with it. But that's another thing that has to be said about the *Jüdische Gemeinde*: once they do decide to accept you, they are extremely helpful and supportive, no matter what your political orientation is. In fact within the *Gemeinde* itself the political spectrum is quite broad. And you can't imagine how important this was for me at the time. In the GDR when you apply for an exit visa, your whole world rejects you: you lose your job, you lose your Party membership (I had been a member of the SED), your friends, etc. There I was suddenly all alone, and the Jews put themselves out to take care of me: the Cantor, Irene Runge and Peter Kirchner especially. For me, joining the *Jüdische Gemeinde* was a gesture of thanks as well as a concretization of my Jewish identity and feeling of belonging.

R.O. Does that mean that before you applied for your exit visa you never really lived as a Jew?

T.E. No.

R.O. Was your wife Jewish?

T.E. There are no Jewish women in the GDR.

R.O. What about Sophia Kahn?*

T.E. My God, Sophia! She's going to be a grandmother soon!

R.O. Do you have any children?

T.E. No. In the GDR whether or not you're Jewish is totally irrelevant socially. Being Jewish means you come from a household where a couple

---

*Pseudonym

of traditions are still observed, and where certain special foods are eaten on the holidays. On the bookshelf there are usually a couple of very old Hebrew dictionaries and the one or the other ritual object so that you know you're Jewish, and that's it. There is no Jewish education and no pressure to become a member of the *Jüdische Gemeinde*. To the contrary, as I've told you, it's just about impossible to join the *Gemeinde*. When my grandfather was a boy, he went to *Jüdische Knabenschule* (Jewish boys' school), but we don't have that any more either. How can you learn about the tradition and religion?

In the GDR I felt no need to join the *Jüdische Gemeinde* to demonstrate opposition to anything, and I had no practical use for it either. It just happened that, at the age of thirty, I needed a job. But I'm not religious, and I have no intention of ever becoming religious. I want to join the *Jüdische Gemeinde* here, in West Berlin, learn some Hebrew, and go to synagogue once in a while, which I see as a cultural thing, not as any kind of religious belief.

R.O. In relation to your joining the *Jüdische Gemeinde*, wanting to learn Hebrew, etc., do you think the older generation of Marxists underestimated people's need for some kind of religious identity?

T.E. One can criticize Marxism for having been, in its practical beginnings and basic presuppositions, some kind of religion. Something developed. There was a theoretical basis upon which a new state structure was to be built. Religion is nothing other than that. It expresses certain kinds of behavioural norms – the ten commandments, etc. Suddenly Marxism had new norms. Marxism faced the task of building a new world on the basis of its materialist, non-idealist *Weltanschauung*. They tried this for about thirty-five years. And after thirty-five, or thirty-four years, you get so disillusioned. What have we actually accomplished? What's there? People say, 'My God! This isn't the way they explained it to us!' And it is a very materialist explanation. Being a Jew is a convenient way out of this. You get back to your roots. Whether that's right or not is another question. But somehow you do get back to your roots, and you distance yourself a bit from Marxism. Not completely. In the GDR you can't free yourself completely from Marxism any more than you can free yourself from being Jewish. But you can get involved with other things. You come back to them.

R.O. You found your way to the *Jüdische Gemeinde* through your lawyer. What about the people who don't have that kind of contact?

T.E. They don't get there. Outsiders have just about no access to the Jewish Community. The *Jüdische Gemeinde* in East Berlin has been basically preparing its own destruction, and they know it. That's one thing I do reproach them with. They really have to be more open and accessible to people, even if that entails the risk that some people will show interest and then stop coming. Many people have tried going to the *Jüdische Gemeinde*, and quit out of frustration. They couldn't stand the members' suspicion – almost hostility – to outsiders.

But you also have to see that many people think it's 'in' to be Jewish. There are rumours of something similar here in West Berlin: that for many people, being a member of the Jewish Community, or being Jewish is chic. I saw a lot of that when I worked at the cemetery. Lots of people who began to take an interest in Jewishness and in Jewish traditions. Sometimes you got the impression that they were doing it as a kind of legitimate opposition to the state. In the GDR we have an expression: 'The Jews in the GDR are a "protected species".' Because of this I can understand somewhat the closure of the *Jüdische Gemeinde* in East Berlin: their reluctance to become a sanctuary for everyone who feels frustrated with current GDR policy or with Marxism.

The other problem that would arise in the absorption of many new members is an adminstrative one. As you know. the *Gemeinde* has no cadres of full-time administrators. The President and Vice-President both have full-time jobs. There's a woman who administers the old age home, the kosher meat store, and the cemeteries: she's a full-time employee, but she's not Jewish. And you can imagine the time and energy it would take to screen a lot of new people and decide who is Jewish, who isn't, and why they want to join. And, of course, the *Jüdische Gemeinde* in East Berlin doesn't want to give the impression of being a gathering place for people who oppose the state. You know, it's so complicated, I was thinking about that recently and it would almost be a reason to distance myself from the *Gemeinde* again just to dissociate myself from the chicness of being Jewish and from the opportunism that's also sometimes involved.

R.O. What advantages are there to being Jewish in the GDR?

T.E. Mostly career advantages. Just like here in West Berlin, lots of public institutions like the radio and television stations are happy to have a Jew around to show that they're not anti-Semitic.

R.O. You mean a 'house Jew'.

T.E. Exactly. I should add that there are many Jews in the GDR whose families were Jewish, who have severed their ties to religion, but are nonetheless Jewish. The *Jüdische Gemeinde* is really very small, and membership in the *Gemeinde* (or lack of it) does not mean that you are or aren't Jewish. You know there are many Jewish politicians in the GDR. And many Jews have no contact with the *Gemeinde* but are sympathizers. When the *Gemeinde* needs something, these people are there to help, though it would never occur to any of them to join or to be religious.

R.O. Does being a member of the *Jüdische Gemeinde* in East Berlin have any particular social connotations?

T.E. No. It has absolutely no relation to prestige.

R.O. Are many members of the *Gemeinde* religious?

T.E. I'm not sure yet how it is in the West, but in East Berlin you don't assume that most of the people who go to religious services believe in God, or are religious. The President of the *Jüdische Gemeinde* doesn't have to be religious, and if you watch him when he goes up to the Torah, you'll see that he can read Hebrew, but not that well.

R.O. Is that just him, or is it politically important that he not be religious?

T.E. I don't know. The role of the *Jüdische Gemeinde* in East Berlin is in no way comparable to that of Jewish Communities in the West. In East Berlin being a member of the *Jüdische Gemeinde* does not necessarily mean that one is religious. It is basically the only chance to be among Jews, to talk about certain things. It also has something to do with the past. When you go to services or to a concert there, you feel like you're among your own kind, among people who have a similar fate. That doesn't necessarily mean becoming obsessed with your fate or with the past, but the past is still with us. And when you meet your Jewish friends once a week, or over the High Holidays, you legitimate and renew your ties to this past.

Of course in the GDR you don't have a situation where you have to be concerned about anti-Semitism on a daily basis. Officially there is no anti-Semitism in the GDR and the little that there is, is in no way comparable to the anti-Semitism I've read about here in the West. The only open political differences that the Jewish Communities in the GDR have with the government are expressed in the newspaper published by the Jewish Communities, and they involve press coverage of the Middle East conflict. Sentences like 'Israel pursues its Final Solution of the Lebanon Question' are unacceptable to Jews and the Jews make their objections known. The Israelis can pursue bad policies, but in no instance should one bring words like 'final solution' or 'exterminate' into the argument, though it happens often. But this in no way constitutes official anti-Semitism; it's just that to a Jew certain words and certain lines of argument are provocative, and shouldn't have to be dealt with. But this is basically the only problem that Jews have in the GDR. And it doesn't lead automatically to the kind of self-defence organization that one sees among Jews in the West. Here, in West Berlin, Jews often get together to collectively oppose particular threats such as anti-Semitism, anti-foreigner sentiment or policies, or even a particular policy of the state of Israel. In the GDR these problems barely exist, so there's no need for self-defence or oppositional organizing. In the GDR when someone says, 'Why don't you come to the *Jüdische Gemeinde*', they're inviting you to come and learn more about your cultural and political past; to remember that part of your family was killed by the Nazis and that you are also a Jew. But there's no pressure. Do you understand the difference?

Helmut Eschwege

13 The Unorthodox View of Jewish History in the German Democratic Republic*

Helmut Eschwege (*interviewed by Hajo Funke*)

Helmut Eschwege is the German Democratic Republic's major authority on modern Jewish history. In 1966 he edited *Kennzeichen J: Bilder, Dokumente, Berichte zur Geschichte der Verbrechen des Hitlerfaschismus an den deutschen Juden*, (East Berlin), the first comprehensive document-ation of the destruction of German Jewry under Hitler to be published in the GDR. When, in the late 1960s, Eschwege's study of the German Jewish anti-Fascist Resistance was rejected for publication in his own country, he sent it on to the Leo Baeck Institute in London. It was published in a shortened form in English in the *Leo Baeck Institute Year Book*, Vol. XV (1970) under the title 'Resistance of German Jews against the Nazi Regime' (pp. 143–80)[1]. This work was later elaborated, refined and published in German as a book co-authored with Konrad Kwiet, *Selbstbehauptung und Widerstand: Deutsche Juden im Kampf um Existenz und Menschenwürde 1933–1945* (Hans Christians Verlag, Hamburg, 1984). Eschwege's other major work is *Die Synagoge in der deutschen Geschichte: Eine Dokumentation* (Dresden, 1980).

When I requested permission to interview Mr Eschwege in summer 1984, I was told it was impossible to reach him at that time (which was not unlikely). But when the next year I again requested permission – two months ahead of the proposed date – my letter was neither acknowledged nor answered. At about this time I heard that Hajo Funke, a West German political scientist and journalist, had taped an interview with Eschwege in West Berlin in early autumn 1983. Dr Funke was kind enough to contribute his cassette to my research project on Jews in the GDR. The translation and editing are mine.

*This interview was originally published in *New German Critique*, Spring – Summer 1986.

H.E. My father came from the Alsace, my mother from Halberstadt. I was born in Hanover. My father, though of German Jewish origins, was very religious, so in 1918, after the First World War, the family moved to Hamburg so that the children could attend the Jewish school, the Talmud Torah, there. We had no Jewish school in Hanover.

The Talmud Torah was a *Realschule*, a technical–commercial school. There wasn't too much religion there. Rather, we studied Hebrew; we learned to read the prayer book and, eventually, other texts too. We were also exposed to some basic concepts, but we never learned to read difficult texts or to speak Hebrew; that was never the idea. What we got was basic preparation for participating in prayer services. In religious studies we also read the Bible which is a history book for Jews in a way that it isn't for Christians – that's why in Israel they learn the Bible by heart. Years later, when I went to Israel, I thought I would be able to make myself understood in Hebrew; but in the end I had to relearn the language, though I did have the basic concepts to build on.

Hundreds of Jewish children from Orthodox families attended this Talmud Torah; children living in Hamburg and also in towns up to 40 km away. But there were some non-Jewish teachers, and we had a very good German history teacher who awakened my interest in history and geography while I was still very young; and this became important for my later work.   Naturally there was no anti-Semitism in the school, but as soon as we left the school building, or even went out in the playground, there were constant fist fights with non-Jewish children. I remember when I was 6, 7, 8 years old, we went out on the street only with our parents; many of the neighbourhoods in which the Jews lived were also inhabited by the German *petite bourgeoisie*, and they were, of course, strongholds of the National Socialists and other conservative groups.

H.F. Already in the 1920s?

H.E. In the early 1920s there were already many very reactionary and anti-Semitic groups, and there were no Christian youth groups that tried to work with the Jews and help them as one finds today. As soon as you walked out of your house, the non-Jewish children would start calling you names – '*Jude, etzi Lebertran*' (Jew, Bah, Codliver oil) – and all kinds of little songs that they sang. By the time I was ten or twelve years old, constant fist fights had become the norm.

H.F. Is that why you learned boxing?

H.E. I learned boxing later when I entered vocational school. By that time I was sixteen, and the fights had become much more serious and bloody. We all learned boxing then because we had to be able to defend ourselves. And this wasn't only in Hamburg, but in many cities: and the end of it was that we became politically organized very early because we had to find outside help. Some of us joined the Communist youth group; I joined the Social Democratic youth group – it was called the *Jungbanner* – when I was sixteen.

After 1929 things got very nasty. There was an enormous amount of street fighting, not only Jews against anti-Semites, but also Social Democrats and Communists against the Nazis. And, at that point, the Jews still had it relatively good, because since the Jews were well organized and stuck together, they suffered less unemployment than the Germans. And the children were all organized in Jewish youth groups. It was only after vocational training that we joined non-Jewish organizations. And then the choice was limited. For example, in Hamburg at that time there was a Social Democratically-oriented city-wide parents' association with representatives from each school. My father was one of the five representatives from the Jewish school. My father was not a member of the Social Democratic Party, but, since everything to the right of the Social Democrats was very conservative and anti-Semitic, he could be active only in a Social Democratic organization.

By the time I was in vocational school, the situation had become much more serious. The conservatives and the Nazis were now well organized – the schoolchildren in the *Stahlhelm*, and the older boys in the SA (Storm Troops). The *Jungdeutsche Orden* wasn't quite so anti-Semitic, but it wasn't very strong either. Hamburg was then a Social Democratic stronghold, but the Social Democrats weren't strong in the areas where the Jews lived.

The German Jews had slowly become accustomed to the situation, so we still didn't think of leaving, though the Polish Jews had begun to get the idea that things were getting continually worse. Around 1930 the major Jewish organizations – for example, the Jewish wire service and the Jewish writers' association which had their headquarters in Berlin – began to leave the country and move either to the East or to the West because they sensed that it was becoming impossible to carry on in Germany. Jewish capital too had begun to relocate beyond the German borders. The Warburg family had already opened up a branch office in Holland – and perhaps in other countries as well – even though the Warburgs were members of the conservative *Deutsche Volkspartei*.

During this time I completed my three years of vocational training. My father then suggested that, because of the massive unemployment, I should take a fourth year of training. I did half of the fourth year, and then I left and headed south for Switzerland. I was still under-age, and my father called me back to Germany, and packed me off to a religious agricultural school in Fulda. This turned out to be a very religious place and I didn't last there for too long. This was in 1933, and by then the Jewish Community had opened an agricultural school in Hamburg to train Jewish adolescents for emigration; and I enrolled there.

Many young Jews were preparing to leave Germany at this time. The Nazi harassment was enormous. There was a massive desecration of Jewish cemeteries, smashing display windows of Jewish stores, and the boycott of Jewish businesses had been called, so the economic situation of the Jews had begun to deteriorate. I should also say something about the Jewish youth groups, of which there was a very large number representing a wide variety of Jewish political orientations. There were several Zionist youth groups; there was the CV (Central Verein), or German–Jewish youth who weren't Zionists, but, like the Bund in the East, they were oriented toward local problems; and there were also religious youth groups and other youth groups which were more like hiking clubs.

H.F. You're talking about the rabid anti-Semitism that began in 1933?

H.E. No. There was rabid anti-Semitism before 1933. There was significant anti-Semitism already at the turn of the century, but it became much more intense during the Weimar period. Right after the First World War the Germans began to blame the Jews for the defeat. They started talking about the *Dolchstoss*, the stab in the back that the Jews had supposedly perpetrated against the Germans, causing them to lose the war; and large sectors of the German population actually believed this. And, with the exception of the Democratic Party, the Social Democratic Party, and the Communists, all the political parties were anti-Semitic, even the *Volkspartei* which had some Jews in it – for example, Stresemann's[2] wife was Jewish. In 1930 the Democratic Party united with the *Jungdeutsche Orden*, a completely reactionary organization, and that made things even more difficult for the Jews.

H.F. How do you explain this increase in anti-Semitism during the Weimar period?

H.E. There was always latent anti-Semitism in Germany which was cultivated in part by the Church. The precursors of the Nazis were also clergy, and the Jews had always functioned as a lightning rod, so naturally, the defeat in the First World War was attributed to them. The Germans even had the gall to do a census of Jews in the military during the war. They wanted to show that the Jews were draft dodgers, but the project backfired because in the end it demonstrated that the Jews lost as many men as the Germans, if not more. But that didn't stop the anti-Semitic agitation. As unemployment increased, it too was blamed on the Jews; so that, with the exception of the Social Democratic and Communist youth groups, there was hardly a German organization that would admit Jews. That's why the Jews developed their own organizations within the Jewish community.

Also important in the Weimar period is that, in contrast to Christians,

Jews who considered themselves free thinkers didn't leave the Jewish Community, perhaps because the Jewish Community offered a certain protection against the anti-Semitic environment, and perhaps also because the anti-Semites made no distinction between religious and non-religious Jews, so there was nothing to be gained from leaving the Jewish Community. In fact, on the contrary, once the Nazis came to power, many Jews who had left the Jewish Community rejoined it, so that already in the Weimar period, even the very large synagogues were short of seats for the High Holidays; though, except for the Orthodox, most German Jews went to synagogue only on the High Holidays, or not even that often. Today Israel has become the substitute for religion; in the Weimar years most Jews were no longer religious, but they maintained their membership in the Jewish Community.

H.F. How is it that you didn't become religious like your parents?

H.E. It probably had to do with my early involvement with the Social Democrats. In 1933 the people I met at the Jewish agricultural school in Hamburg were a very mixed group; there were young doctors and lawyers as well as artisans – all preparing to emigrate. I spent a year there, and then I too left Germany for Denmark where there was no anti-Semitism because there were hardly any Jews. But I had to leave after six weeks because I was working with the Social Democratic youth group there. On the advice of Jewish friends who had come to Denmark from Russia during the time of the Czar, I fled to Latvia.

In the early 1930s there was a campaign to persuade Jews to emigrate to Birobidjan, the Jewish colony in the Soviet Union, as an alternative to Palestine; and large numbers of Jews from all over Europe were heading there. A lot of my friends in Hamburg had already left for Birobidjan, so I didn't think twice about going there too. But when I got to Latvia, the border had already been closed. Since it was impossible to continue on to Birobidjan, I went instead to Estonia.

With hindsight, that saved my life, because not a single German Jew survived in Birobidjan. I later met a couple of Jews from other parts of Europe who left Birobidjan in 1937, but the German Jews weren't allowed to leave. When the war began, they all simply disappeared. The Soviets probably turned them over to the Nazis along with other German emigrants. People in Hamburg have tried to find out what happened to these German Jews and, on trips to the Soviet Union after the war, I also attempted many times to learn at least something of their fate, but with no success at all.

I had been given two addresses in Latvia. At the first address, a young man opened the door and said to me: 'Listen, the police are right upstairs. Last night the Fascists took over. Do you have another address?' So I went to the second address, the home of a blind lawyer who was a leading personality in the party. He advised me to travel on to Estonia where the Fascists weren't in power; they had recently won an electoral majority, but had been barred from taking over, and the Zionist youth organization *Hashomer Hazair* could help me.

In Estonia I learned Yiddish, and I familiarized myself with East European Jewish culture. I was in Tallinn which was then called Reval; they had a Jewish theatre there and lots of lectures and readings. I had no work permit, but the Estonians are very decent people, and they let me work anyway. Every seven weeks, though, I had to cross the border to Finland to renew my residence permit.

Estonia was an incredibly poor country: the people there were living in conditions we know about only through Maxim Gorki's short stories. In my two and a half years there I never slept alone in a bed except once for six or seven days when I contracted jaundice. But in spite of the fact that people lived poorly and earned little, one felt good there because of the cultural and social life which was much richer than that I had known in Germany. There were many Jewish organizations – some Zionist and others less Zionist. Altogether it was very exciting. And in Estonia, too, I joined the Social Democratic and Jewish youth groups.

Of course there were also negative things. The whole country was infested with fleas; and life in all the hotels as well was a constant struggle with these vermin. But after two years I got used to them and they seemed to have gotten used to me too. At the end of the two and a half years I got permission to emigrate to Palestine, through relatives who were already there. I travelled to Palestine via Sweden, Denmark, Holland, Belgium, and Switzerland.

When I first arrived in Palestine, I went to the German kibbutz Chugim in Raananah which I had already contacted from Estonia. They sent me to a different work-site every four weeks. I did four weeks at the Dead Sea, four weeks at Bat Yam where they were starting to build a Jewish city, then four weeks here and four weeks there. This lasted about a year, and then they threw me out because I had ties to left-wing organizations that were suspected of being Communist.

H.F. But if the kibbutzim had a socialist orientation, why did they throw you out?

H.E. Under Stalin the Soviets had begun to cruelly persecute Zionists. All the Zionist organizations in the Soviet Union were dissolved and their members were sent to Siberia. Consequently the kibbutzim were not anti-Communist – in fact they had a Communist orientation from the beginning – but they weren't very pro-Soviet. And at that time the number of Communists in Palestine was actually quite high.

I then went to Kibbutz Hefzibah, an older, more settled kibbutz which had been founded by Jews from the Sudetenland and Bessarabia. They spoke German, and I was quite happy there for a year. When I first arrived at Hefzibah, the kibbutz was involved in a conflict with the trade union confederation, the Histadrut; and, as part of the conflict, the Histadrut was withholding its labour. A year later, though, an agreement was reached. At that time I was in the hospital with typhus. The leader of the kibbutz came to visit me there, and he explained: 'We've made peace with the Histadrut, and they've stipulated only one condition – that you can't work with us any more. But don't worry, we were very satisfied with you. You were thrown out of the first kibbutz overnight; we'll give you time to get your things together, we'll give you some clothing and, if there's something we can do for you, we'll do it.' I told him that my mother was still in Germany and, even though the British had already cut off immigration, he got her a visa within three days. This was already in early 1939, after *Kristallnacht*.

At that time we weren't Israelis; our passport was stamped 'Palestine'. The Jews used to call it, not a 'Palestin-ian' passport but a 'Palestin-nigger' passport, because it was a colonial pass. We could use it everywhere except in England. By this time my German passport was no longer valid: the German embassy hadn't renewed it. After leaving Hefzibah, I took a series of different jobs, and at times I earned good money too.

I also belonged to the SAP (Socialist German Workers Party), the only German Jewish Communist organization in Palestine, and to the Communist Party of Palestine. They were orthodox Communists and we were quite a large group. When war broke out between the Soviet Union and Finland, there were vehement discussions about whether or not the Soviet Union was justified in widening its territory into Finland to protect Leningrad which had previously been only 50 km from the border – the Finns had already cost the Soviets any number of armies. There was a lot of indignation about that in Palestine and elsewhere, though today we understand it, and Israel itself maintains that Tel Aviv has to be 50 km – and not 15 km – from the border.

In those days too, the German anti-Fascist, Communist, and Social Democratic propaganda was maintaining that the Germans were wrecking their economy through excessive rearmament, and that it would never come to war. So I said to myself: 'If that's the case, Sweden is closer to Germany than Palestine'. I had earned enough money, so I hopped on a ship and went to Estonia and then Finland, but no one was getting into Sweden. I waited a while in Finland, but meanwhile the Germans occupied Danzig, formerly an independent city, and I decided to go back to Palestine. With hindsight I don't regret the Communist propaganda and the aborted move to Sweden because on the way back to Palestine, which took me through Czernowitz, Buchowina, Lodz, Warsaw, and Wilna, I got to know Jewish life in Bessarabia which I wouldn't like to have missed.

I got back to Palestine at the beginning of the bitter years of the war. The Germans had sealed off the Mediterranean Sea, so there was no import and no export. That precipitated a time of high unemployment. The British began to withdraw from Egypt where they had their major military installations, and where Rommel had begun to stake out his territory. The Italians were trying to press north from Abyssinia, and, in Syria and Lebanon, to the north of (what became) Israel, the French troops joined the Vichy government, that is, the Nazis.

The situation began to heat up. The British moved their entire military depots north to Palestine, and that helped the employment situation a bit. They then tried to march north to Beirut. When they were repelled by the French, they brought in the *Haganah*, the Jewish defence groups.

The whole time that I was in Palestine there was civil war – at times very intense. It was a triangular conflict: the Jews against the Arabs, the Jews against the British, and also the Arabs against the British. The British had a massive police force all over Palestine – they had almost every hill covered – and there were British and Jewish soldiers, and Jewish and Arab police. So, at Hefzibah, for example, which was at the foot of Mount Gilboa, the Arabs would come down and start shooting. In the next town the British heard that there was shooting and that the Jews had defended themselves and they got into their jeeps to come over. But immediately someone would call the kibbutz from the police station, and warn us to hide our weapons because the British were on their way. Both the Jews and the Arabs were then using weapons stolen from the British police.

Despite that kind of support, guard duty in this civil war was not pleasant. In Israel the night is pitch black, and you can't see your hand in front of your face, so that in this war, most of the Jewish casualties were killed by Jews, and the Arab victims, by Arabs. No one dared call out: 'Who's there', because the other would have shot first. You just couldn't see a thing in that darkness.

H.F. Do you think this war between the Jews and the Arabs was avoidable, or was it a necessary consequence of the Zionist idea?

H.E. It was not avoidable. The Jews had bought large tracts of land from the Arab Effendis, large landowners who sat on the Riviera or wherever while Arab tenant farmers worked their land. And, once the land was sold, the tenant farmers were unemployed. And the situation got continually worse.

H.F. Could the unemployment among Arab tenant farmers have been avoided?

H.E. They could have avoided it, but they didn't want to. They wanted Jews to have work, and there were constant strikes to force Jewish landowners to hire Jewish rather than Arab workers on construction sites because the Jews also needed work. The paradox is that today there isn't a single Jewish construction worker in Israel. All the construction in Tel Aviv, Haifa, etc. is done by Palestinians. Even the Jewish villages being built in the Palestinian territories are being built by Palestinian constuction workers.

H.F. And that gave the Arabs a justification for intensifying the conflict?

H.E. The Arab reaction is completely understandable. As a labour force they felt constantly threatened.

H.F. But couldn't all this have been anticipated and avoided?

H.E. No, because even the Labour Party participated in the boycott of Arab labour. They not only participated, they probably also partly organized it. And the justification was the same kind of purely chauvinistic argument they use today: the Jews need the work.

H.F. Did you critize this policy at the time?

H.E. The Communists were naturally against the boycott of Arab labour, on the one hand; but, on the other hand, they also profited from it because it meant work for their people. In the end it meant that after 1939, the Jews and the Arabs each had their own Communist Party,[3] and that situation prevailed until after the Second World War. The civil war made it impossible for them to work together in one party. There were even a few villages where Jews and Arabs lived together peacefully during the day, and started shooting each other at sundown. Once the Second World War started, however, the civil war abated somewhat.

By 1942 or '43 the British were starting to build up their forces and, as a result of the high unemployment, the Jews began to volunteer for the British army. They were trained with broomsticks and similar equipment: there were hardly any weapons. The Zionists, though, were calling for a Jewish boycott of British military service. They wanted the Jews to fight in their own units. In the end, the *Haganah* prepared the way north to Lebanon for the British. They probably got their weapons from East Africa. Enormous numbers of troops were then coming to Palestine from East Africa, South Africa and Australia to fight Rommel and to fight the Italians in Abyssinia and Somalia.

On the Italian front there was basically no war: most of the Italians deserted, so it wasn't very bloody. And Rommel's campaign fell apart because his tanks had no cooling system – as the British tanks had – and his men broiled in the heat. They got as far as the Egyptian border, but then it was all over: that was a stroke of luck for the British.

Meanwhile the Germans had stationed themselves on Crete, and started to bomb Palestine which had no anti-aircraft installations. So the British began to build airports and supply bases: 1942 marked the beginning of the big military era in Palestine. The Russians mobilized there for the Soviet army; the Greeks and Yugoslavs were mobilizing armies there too. Palestine was becoming a centre of troop concentration for the Mediterranean, from which units were to be sent to Greece and Italy. The Czechs put together a division of Czechoslovakian Jews in Palestine, and the Poles came too with their entire army, at least – anti-Semites every one of them. They made pogroms against their own troops in Palestine, and then the Jews fled. They were terrible.

As a Communist, I volunteered to fight with the Russians. I presented myself at their recruitment office, and the following conversation took place:

They: Mr Eschwege, it's nice that you've come to us. What is your citizenship?

I: I'm German, but I had to leave Germany because I'm a Jew.

They: As far as we're concerned, you're a Jew. We don't make any distinctions. A Jew is a Jew. Would you be perhaps also a member of the Communist Party?

I: Yes.

They: Then why don't you go over to the British. You're more important to us there than here.

H.F. You mean they wanted to plant you in the British army as an agent?

H.E. No, they just thought it was a good idea to have a couple of Communists in the British army. The Communist Party was then very weak in England. Besides which the British had a very democratic army; it was fantastic. So, in that way I came to volunteer for the British army. I was still an auxiliary policeman with the British, and I must have looked sort of sad. The German bombing continued and there were no air raid shelters. I lost a lot of relatives in those raids. The houses were all very flimsy, two or three storeys at most, and everything was still very primitive. There was no highway then from Tel Aviv to Haifa; you had to drive through sand dunes.

The British were very kind to me. They made me a salesman for their airport construction division. I took a short trip to Italy for them, and a short trip to Egypt. Then they put me in charge of a smoke-screening installation near Haifa where there was a large refinery. We never knew what this installation was for, or whether it was meant to be used against the Russians. But it never functioned; it just cost the British a lot of money.

At the end of the war I was demobilized and, having no occupation, I went, at the first opportunity, to the Czechoslovakian embassy. Goldsticker, the man who was then serving as Consul, later became president of the writers' organization and played a very important role in the Slansky trials. I got permission to go to Czechoslovakia – for medical treatment, naturally – and I stayed there for six months. It was there that I first learned about what had happened in Germany during the Nazi years. I was also surprised that the Czechs were angry at the anti-Fascists and not at the Nazis. Little by little it became clear that when the Nazis invaded, almost all the Czech Communists and Social Democrats defected to them, betraying and selling each other in the process; though before the war the best Communists and Social Democrats in Czechoslovakia – the leaders at all the Congresses – were Germans.

From Czechoslovakia I went on to Dresden. I had any number of friends – in fact I had brought a list of 250 Germans – who wanted to settle in the Eastern Zone, and some of them had lived in Dresden. I didn't have any relatives left in Hamburg, so I also went to Dresden. It turned out, however, that neither the German Communists nor our Russian friends had any interest in Jews, nor, most probably, in any immigrants from the Western emigration who were to them already half agents.

When I first got to Dresden, as a precaution, I arranged to live in a house next door to the Soviet Headquarters. From there I could look around and see how the situation was for the Jews. I started to work in the SED, in the provincial administration. For the first six months I still ran around in my British army uniform which was very convenient: I could come and go as I pleased. Then I worked for the district cultural commission, building libraries; and after that I created an archive of the working class movement for the province. My next project was with the Museum of German History, but then came a series of Party proceedings that went on for five years. I was thrown out of the Party three or four times because I had been in the Western emigration and that, naturally, made me angry.

The Slansky trials played a very important role in my life. Slansky and the other victims were almost all Jews and, for that reason, they were accused of being agents – of Tito, of the US, and of at least twenty other states. Being Jewish was turned into an accusation. In the earlier show trials in Bulgaria it had been demonstrated that anyone who survived a concentration camp must have collaborated with the Nazis. Then in the trial of Rajk[4] in Hungary, they proved that the veterans of the Spanish Civil War were also agents, so all the Jews who had fought in Spain were executed.

And similar things happened in the German Democratic Republic. There were trials; Jews were imprisoned; and most of the Jews fled, including the Boards of Directors of all the Jewish Communities here. There was a certain anti-Jewish hysteria and I suffered a lot under it, though in the end I was lucky. It was through this experience that I began to get interested in Jewish history. I said to myself: 'Write, study Jewish history, show them what the Nazis did, and they can see it's the same thing.' Since then I've written many books on the subject, though I've never had a university education.

H.F. You mentioned that it was in Czechoslovakia that you first learned what happened to the Jews in Germany under Hitler. How did you react to that?

H.E. Well, an enormous number of non-Jews and Communists were also killed. And there was violent anti-Semitism in the Soviet Union after the war under Stalin. When I first came to Dresden, whole groups within the Soviet army consisted entirely of Jews; for example, all the cultural and political officers were Jews. At first I didn't understand it, but then I found out that because of the anti-Semitism in the Soviet Union, many Jews didn't demobilize after the war, but remained in the army because they felt more secure there – Tschukow, for example, was protected by the military. This was especially true of Jews from the Ukraine where the anti-Semitism was truly terrible.

In Dresden I realized that the Germans, too, were all more or less influenced by the Nazis, even those who had been in concentration camps and in the punitive battalions in the military. In the early years they all thought they could desert, but the longer the war dragged on, the more fanatic Nazis they became, especially when they realized that they could no longer defect.

H.F. How do you explain that?

H.E. They were afraid of the Russians. They had seen the way the Germans had treated prisoners and the civilians in the territories they occupied, and that gave them some idea of the revenge the Russians might take.

I ultimately moved into a working-class neighbourhood in Dresden. Before Hitler, the people there had all been Communists and Social Democrats, but they were never nearly as numerous as they seemed. The Nazis used to like to hang flags, so the Communists hung twice as many flags – not only from every house, but from every window. There are also impressive statistics about the thousands, even hundreds of thousands of Communists who were in jails and concentration camps; but the truth of the matter is that many of them were imprisoned three or four times, so the actual number of individuals involved was much smaller.

Today we know that as soon as a dictatorship comes to power, it has the masses behind it. It is only when the weaknesses become visible that the opposition can rebuild and try to topple it, as we can see in Chile and Greece where, typically, a dictator was deposed by his own people because his economic and political programmes fell apart. Terror is a powerful instrument that dictators have at their disposal.

H.F. People are also fascinated by dictators.

H.E. Naturally, but in Germany the enormous casualties and the suffering could have tipped the scales in the other direction. But the time wasn't ripe, and people were afraid of the victors.

In Dresden I got married, had three children, and then I got stuck there.

H.F. Do you feel comfortable in Dresden?

H.E. Well, little by little I've won myself a certain freedom. I write my books and they're published outside the GDR. And even before my retirement I could travel abroad.[5] You just don't put up with any flak and it's OK.

I have more freedom than most people here, but I can't say that I'm happy to live here and not in West Germany or elsewhere, or that I'm a really enthusiastic citizen of the GDR.

H.F. What's your greatest fear when you think of Germany?

H.E. I'm afraid that if tomorrow the Soviet Union would hold trials against Jews because they're Zionists – which is completely possible – then the GDR would do the same.

H.F. And what kinds of fears do you have regarding West Germany?

H.E. I have fewer fears regarding West Germany. Naturally Jews in West Germany are afraid of Palestinian terrorists, and there are attacks on Jews there, but [in West Germany] the Jews can defend themselves. In [East Germany] they can't.

H.F. And what is the message of your story for the younger generation?

H.E. That one must always be alert and question those in power. You know, yesterday I saw on television a debate between a prominent Austrian Conservative and the leader of the Socialist youth movement in Austria who announced that his group was planning to demonstrate the next day with the Communists against nuclear weapons. The Conservative questioned the appropriateness of such a demonstration in a country like Austria which has no nuclear weapons. The Socialist replied that whether or not Austria possesses its own nuclear weapons, when the atom bombs fall over Europe, Austrians will suffer all the same. And the situation is exactly the same in the German Democratic Republic. Officially we have no nuclear weapons, but when the Soviets release their rockets, they'll fall on our villages too. And it's not just the issue of nuclear weapons, but with other questions as well. One must be alert these days, and one must try to be politically active.

14 Afterword
The German Democratic Republic and its Jewish Community

As mentioned in the introduction, this research project was conceptualized and carried out as a preliminary study, to generate questions, hypotheses, and models: it was never seen as a comprehensive or a definitive work, and the judgements ventured in the following pages should be seen as tentative rather than conclusive. Particularly, the fact that ten of the twelve interviews were conducted in East Berlin, but most of the documentation was found in West Berlin and New York, introduces a methodological bias. It is hoped that the German Democratic Republic will consider making its own archives more accessible to Western researchers in the near future to facilitate the development of a less biased and more refined analysis.

Because of Germany's Nazi past, the Jewish question in the GDR is much more important than local demography would suggest; it goes to the root of national identity – and this is true of West Germany as well. Beyond the problems of historiography and sociology in the shadow of the 'Iron Curtain', the texts of the twelve interviews reveal that, despite the obvious limitations of Jewish life in the GDR, there are still many ways and styles of being Jewish there, and there are several approaches to many Jewish issues which individuals and functionaries are able and willing to articulate.

Some recurrent themes expressed directly and indirectly in the interviews are:

(a) Whatever may have occurred in the early 1950s, today Jews in the GDR are protected by the state, and are, in fact, a privileged minority.

(b) Despite official denials, anti-Semitism does exist in the GDR, but on a much smaller scale than in many Western European countries, such as West Germany, Austria, and France.

(c) Among Jews who have had a traditional Jewish upbringing, membership in the Jewish Community and interest in things Jewish represents a continuation of the way they have always lived. For some individuals who grew up in Nazi Germany in mixed marriages, a strong Jewish identification can serve as a link with their families' suffering under the Nazis. And for some Jews who were for many years close to the SED – which has always maintained a fiercely secular and internationalist orientation – interest in Judaism provides a way of distancing themselves from the Party without in any way opposing it.

(d) Where in Western Europe one of the major strains within the Jewish community is found in the conflict between the Orthodox and Liberal tendencies – in North America between the Orthodox, Conservative, and Reform movements – in the GDR the main break is between the Jews in the *Jüdische Gemeinde* and the Jews in the SED.

The twelve interviewees also pointed to several problems faced by Jews in the GDR. Some – for example, the definition of a Jew and the personal suffering of individuals caught in the interstices of the rules – are found and have become the subject of public debate in Western Europe, Israel, and North America as well.

The uneasiness stemming from the constant exposure to the local Nazi past would have to be confronted in any polity founded on the ashes of the Third Reich. In West Germany this subject was for a long time suppressed,[1] and in the GDR it was defined away. Clara Berliner reminded me that: 'Here, we are the victors.' But human nature is complicated, and the ghost of Nazism is stubborn and not that easily exorcised. In the words of the East German Jewish writer Stefan Hermlin:

> And then our propagandists thought of applying the unusual expression 'Victors of History', an idea which is in itself absurd because there never are Victors of History and there never have been...every citizen of the GDR could now consider himself a Victor of History. Flattering the people and unburdening them also made it easier to govern. In the long run it is difficult to govern people who feel in some way guilty. With this formulation, the GDR achieved a certain political authority.
>
> Unfortunately even many comrades [i.e. Party members] say, with a certain self satisfaction, we have overcome the past, *they* [i.e. Germans in the BRD] haven't, they're still struggling with it. No one has the right to say that. (Hermlin, 1983, pp. 399–400, author's translation)

Sonja Berne and Jalda Rebling, among others, expressed feelings of cultural isolation from Jewish life outside the GDR. This isolation impoverishes Jewish life, but it is not a particularly Jewish phenomenon. The entire population of the GDR is culturally isolated from Western Europe and North America, and this applies to most aspects of life.

Being actively Jewish in the GDR means being part of a respected minority, but it also means being outside the mainstream of public life. Thomas Eckert and Helmut Eschwege became more interested in their Jewishness as they became marginalized within East German society.

Coming directly from the interviews themselves, the observations reviewed above reflect many aspects of the subjective experience of being Jewish in the German Democratic Republic. The Western researcher is then left with the task of constructing from the interviews – and from available documents and historical texts – a hypothesis or model that will illuminate: (a) the events of the early 1950s that led to the formation of the East Berlin Jewish Community, separated from the Jewish Community in West Berlin; (b) the very different situation of Jews in the GDR now; and (c) what one might anticipate for the future.

The North American model of 'ethnicity' – of an immigrant group brought in to augment the unskilled labour force at a time of economic expansion which then settles in and develops an economic and political infrastructure from the basis up – does not apply to the Jewish situation in either post-war Germany. The Jews of East Berlin have no 'ethnic economy', no ethnic kinship system, and no real relationship to a 'homeland'. Dr Hermann Simon is quite correct when he insists that: 'America is very different from the German Democratic Republic, and you can't judge us by what happens there.'

Two years after his interview, Thomas Eckert visited the USA and Canada. When he returned to West Berlin, he wrote up the following notes in the hope of making some of the basic presuppositions of the twelve interviewees more accessible to North American readers.

Since the Romans' expulsion of the Jews from Israel, one finds in literature the concept *'Judenemanzipation'* (Emancipation of the Jews) which conveys the idea of a life of liberation from being without rights and from a life-threatening and miserable dependency on the Jews' respective hosts...(By these criteria) the few Jews living in the GDR have been 'emancipated'.

And the concept of 'emancipation' is found in the works of Marx and Lenin which form the philosophical basis of the GDR...In 1844 Karl Marx published his article, 'On the Jewish Question', with the intention of refuting the position of Bruno Bauer, a German philosopher and early Hegelian who maintained that because Protestantism paved the way for human emancipation, unlike Christians, Jews do not harbour the capability of emancipating themselves.

Marx, by contrast, maintained that Bauer had confused 'human' emancipation with 'political' emancipation. 'Human emancipation will only be complete when the real, individual man...has recognized and organized his own powers *(forces propres)* as *social* powers so that he no longer separates this social power from himself as *political* power'. (Marx, 1984/1963, p. 31.)

Thus in the historical consciousness of the GDR, the socialist transformation of society has taken place (in the GDR). Private property has become social property, and therefore the way to the 'emancipation' of all individuals – including Jews – has been prepared. The continued existence of anti-Semitism in the GDR is considered a relic of past German history, and in no way compromises Marx's conception of 'emancipation' of the Jews through the socialization of production. (Personal correspondence, 5 February 1986, author's translation)

In attempting an analysis of the anti-Jewish campaigns of the early 1950s and the schism that led to the establishment of the *Jüdische Gemeinde* of East Berlin in its present form, a number of points should be kept in mind:

(a) The events, terrible as they were, took place against the background of the Cold War, including the 'show trial' of the Rosenbergs in New York[2] with *its* anti-Semitic implications.

(b) The German Democratic Republic was formally founded in 1949, but it 'gained "independence" from the Soviet Union on 20 September 1955. The official position of the Berlin regime prior to this date reflects the thinking of both the Soviet Zone and the Soviet Union' (Thompson, 1967, p.8). Hence the responsibility of the GDR government for decisions made before 'independence' is debatable.

(c) Jews were not the only segment of GDR society affected by the purges of the eary 1950s.

> In turning against sections of the bureaucracy itself, the apparatus of purge and terror aimed chiefly at those who had independent roots inside the local society. In each country it was the overwhelming majority of the leaders of the underground struggle against the Nazis who were executed or imprisoned, whilst those leaders who had spent the War, and often many years before it, in Moscow were left in sole command. (Harman, 1974/1983, p. 52)

(d) Although allegations that the Jews in the GDR – and especially their leaders – were all 'Zionists, Trotskyists, Imperialist American agents, Titoists, and Cosmopolitans'[3] were clearly hysterical, they were not without some basis in fact. Because of the dimensions of German Jewish emigration in the 1930s and then in the immediate post-war years and the undercurrent of limited return migration after 1949, a disproportionately large fraction of the Jewish population in the GDR had ties to the West.[4] And the international Jewish organizations supplying the Jewish Communities in both Germanys represented Western values and Western interests. Moreover they were working hand-in-glove with the American military. Rabbi Levinson was born in Berlin and was one of the last to escape Nazi Germany in 1941. He returned to Berlin in 1950 and served as Rabbi for the Berlin Jewish Community and as Chaplain for the American Jewish colony until 1953 (Katcher, 1968, pp. 41–4).

The following Memo, dated 21 April 1952, reveals some of the AJDC's concerns and its own conceptualization of its mission in Berlin.

> As Sovietization becomes more all-embracing in the satellite countries and the Iron Curtain more impenetrable...In view of Berlin's role as a mail drop, an office maintained in Germany by the major Jewish organizations could in due course serve as a good listening post, especially for Jewish news emanating from East Germany, Bohemia, Poland, the Baltic countries and the USSR itself. Such news might be forthcoming from local Jewish sources there, or it might be elicited from the assorted intelligence agencies and national DP organizations operating in Western Germany, many of which maintain underground courier service to points in Eastern Europe.
>
> Another eventuality must be mentioned, unpleasant as it is to contemplate. If the Bolshevik regime were to be overthrown or to disintegrate in the next few years, it is to be feared that pogroms would sweep Hungary, Rumania and the Ukraine. An established and well-connected international Jewish representative might then be in a position to exert his influence...(Memorandum to AJDC 20N Letter #800)

(e) Thompson (1967) underlines the role of the new Jewish state in exacerbating an already tense situation.

> Moscow had hoped to extend its influence over the young state of Israel, but was disappointed when Israel emerged as a democratic country patterned after the West: Soviet foreign policy was turning more and more toward supporting and exploiting Arab nationalist movements; and the ardent response of Soviet and satellite Jews to the establishment of Israel had reawakened fears of 'dual loyalty'. (pp. 54–5)

(f) Finally Thompson also points to the social tensions generated by Jewish demands for restitution.

> Apartments, small factories and shops, and personal belongings still remained private property: however, when the Jewish survivors claimed them, they were violently opposed by...those who had

become accustomed to think of former Jewish possessions as their own and of the Jewish survivors as intruders...This group was so large that the Communists and other parties that were still legal defended it against the Jewish claims...This struggle over restitution became accompanied by open or covert anti-Semitic agitation or resulted in an increase of anti-Jewish feelings.

Under this series of pressures, the anti-Jewish terror of the early 1950s served three major purposes. First it destroyed the GDR Jewish Communities as grass roots organizations with their own political basis. The GDR still does not tolerate independent grass roots organizations of any kind. Second, it effected an almost complete separation of its Jews and its Jewish Communities from Western organizations and influences. And third, as the Nazi Aryanization of businesses and professions twenty years previously had demonstrated, the removal of an entire social group from desirable positions – or from the society as a whole – creates new opportunities and the resulting alleviation of some political frustrations for the rest of the population. Once these goals had been achieved, the Jewish Communities in the GDR were allowed to resume many of their activities, i.e. providing specialized services that were in demand and, through their existence, exemplifying their nation's commitment to freedom of religion. And, like other phases of Jewish policy in the GDR, the rehabilitation of the GDR Jewish Communities – albeit in a new form – in June 1953 (three months after Stalin's death) was not a uniquely Jewish phenomenon, but rather part of a whole series of reforms introduced by the SED (Harman, 1974/1983, p. 78). Thus between November 1952 and June 1953 the Jewish Community – and other social groups in the GDR as well – was separated from all other sources of support and attached directly to the East German state on which it is still totally dependent and which it serves.

Thirty-five years after the anti-Jewish campaign of the early 1950s the Jewish Community in East Berlin is not thriving, but it is surviving and receiving generous support from the state – under greatly altered circumstances, among the most important, a relative thaw in the GDR's relations with West Germany and with many other Western countries too. This thaw has permitted the increasing integration of the GDR into the international economy, including the development of tourism as a means of earning Western currency.

East Germany is now a formidable presence in Central Europe. It is the most important source of technology for the Soviet bloc, a major trading partner of both the Federal Republic and the Soviet Union, and through its tariff-free trade with West Germany, a shadow member of the European Economic Community...along with Hungary, it has become the foremost proponent of detente in the Warsaw Pact.

Although a planned visit by Mr. Honecker to Bonn has been postponed, the GDR shows every sign of wanting to expand its contacts with the West. (*The Globe and Mail*, Toronto, 5 October 1984, p. 7)

In the negotiation of trading ties to Western countries, international Jewish organizations are perceived in the GDR as channels of communication and potential mobilizers of local Jewish support in Western countries for trade with the East. From this point of view it is hardly surprising that during the early months of 1986 there were talks between the USA and the GDR concerning the possibility of obtaining 'most favoured nation' status for GDR exports to the USA, and simultaneous negotiations for the export of an American Rabbi to serve in East Berlin.[5] Dr Bela Kiraly, Commander-in-Chief of the Hungarian army in the Nagy government during the 1956 uprising, noted that a similar situation exists in Hungary where 'Kadar has always encouraged Jewish life (in Hungary) to maintain a broad window towards the West.'[6]

In traditional European societies, Jews often functioned as economic middlemen and performers of social and economic 'dirty work'.[7] This niche offered them occasional success at the price of perpetual vulnerability. Arendt (1958) analyses the direct relationship between segments of the Jewish community and various European states in the century before Hitler. In today's Germanys Jews no longer have an economic role: there are too few of them – approximately 30 000 in West Germany and less than 2000 in the GDR – and, as a result of their largely geriatric age distribution and the harm inflicted on them by the Nazis, many Jews are actually expensive dependants. But the Jews of both West and East Germany still have a function. They still serve as middlemen – no longer *economic* but rather *political* middlemen – and they still do 'dirty work'. By their very existence they symbolize and demonstrate the break of the respective German states with the Nazi past, and they serve as links to the Western countries. Bodemann (1983 and 1986) discusses the way in which, starting in 1950, Adenauer initiated negotiations for restitution payments to Jewish victims of Nazism and to the new state of Israel as a central element in his development of a Western-oriented foreign policy for West Germany. In this way the West German Jewish Communities and individual German Jewish emigrants became actively involved as intermediaries in the political and economic reintegration of the BRD into the North American and West European community. The victims of Nazism were made into (and agreed to become) the accomplices of the Nazis' Christian Democratic successors.

Thus, at present, the Jewish Communities in both Germanys have a special relationship to the national government and a special role in the foreign policy of their respective countries. To the extent that anti-Fascism

remains a central component of national identity and trade with the West
– first and foremost with the USA – is expanding and/or thriving, the
Jewish Communities in the GDR and in the BRD can expect popular
and state support. But in the event of a national reconciliation with the
Nazi past and/or a political or economic distancing from the West, the
Jews and the Jewish Communities will suffer. In West Germany, as a
result of the political turn to the right, starting with the election of Kohl
in 1983, and the rising tide of anti-American feeling, the Jews have come
under the increasing pressure of Bitburg, the Korschenbroich scandal,[8]
and the Fassbinder affair in Frankfurt.[9] Gaus (1983) points out that in
the German Democratic Republic, by contrast, anti-Fascism is still the
dominant mood:

> Particularly in comparison with West Germany, it is characteristic
> of East Germans...that they identify with their German state on one
> issue: that the basic, thorough, and complete overcoming of National
> Socialism is an obligation, a concrete ideal which permits no erosion
> through relativising (p. 49, author's translation)

and, despite the deterioration of political relations between the USA and
the USSR, the GDR is still pursuing a policy of integrating into
Western markets. Should these conditions change, there will be negative
repercussions for the entire population of the GDR, but especially for
its Jews.

Postscript
An East–West Simchat Torah, East Berlin, October 1987

After four years of negotiations involving the East German government, the US State Department and the American Jewish Committee, Rabbi Isaac Neumann of Champaign-Urbana, Illinois arrived in East Berlin in early September 1987 to serve as the German Democratic Republic's first Rabbi in twenty-two years. Born in Poland in 1923, Rabbi Neumann lost most of his parental family to the Nazis. Having himself survived Auschwitz, he emigrated to the USA in 1950. Although the costs of Rabbi Neumann's work in East Berlin were originally to have been assumed by the American Jewish Committee, in the end, the East German government agreed to pay the Rabbi a salary too and to provide him with an apartment and a car.

The new American Rabbi was inducted into office on the evening of Rosh Hashanah, the Jewish New Year, in the ornate and lovingly-restored synagogue on the Rykestrasse. Although the Jewish Community of East Berlin numbers fewer than 200 members, the synagogue, which seats over 1000, was filled – with non-affiliated East Berliners from Jewish families, sympathizers and dignitaries representing the governments and churches of both Berlins, complemented by a host of journalists and television camera crews. There was much diversity among the East Berliners. Of the men, some wore dark three-piece suits, others wore jeans and turtlenecks. One young artist had a *kipah* (ritual headcovering) that was an Algerian fez. Many of the women wore wool skirts and sweaters. But a younger woman with red hair had on a peasant blouse and kerchief, a long skirt, and clogs; and an intense-looking woman in her twenties with short dark hair, long white earrings, and blue jeans, nursed her baby in the back row. Standing in the middle of this imposing gathering, I felt I was watching a very new and promising development in Jewish history and in East–West relations.

By the end of September, Rabbi Neumann had organized an informal meeting with members of the Jewish Community and interested non-members to discuss local Jewish needs and interests as a basis for developing cultural programmes. Three hundred people attended, taxing the seating capacity of the hall. Although two-thirds of the members of the Jewish Community are over sixty years old, well over half of the crowd at this meeting were men and women in their twenties, thirties, and forties: students, professionals, academics, and artists. The storekeeper

149

and entrepreneur groups, so prominent in Jewish communities in the West, were missing. With his lively eyes, warm smile, and broken German, Rabbi Neumann radiated energy and *Yiddishkeit*. 'I don't care whether you agree with my views or disagree with them; I don't care whether you like to pray standing up or sitting down, silently or out loud; I don't care whether you think of yourself as Orthodox or Liberal; I'm here to provide the opportunity for us to work together to revive Jewish life in this community...I haven't come here to bring you the truth, but I have a whole supermarket full of ideas for things we can do together.' After this introduction, everyone in the room was with him, including me. Looking especially at those East Berliners born during and after the war, I wondered whether they had ever been told anything like that by anyone. Although the people who came that evening represented very different social groups and Jewish orientations, within ninety minutes plans had been drawn up for a Hebrew language course, an adult reading group, and a two-hour-a-week children's programme. Rabbi Neumann ended the evening by suggesting that, for the next meeting, refreshments be provided for socializing, and perhaps eventually for singing and dancing. Again, despite my problems with the concept of a 'supermarket' of Jewish life in East Berlin, I sensed that something very new and good was beginning to happen.

Over the telephone several days later, Rabbi Neumann invited me to Simchat Torah services on Friday evening. 'But Simchat Torah is Thursday evening, isn't it?' I was confused. 'Well, *we're* going to celebrate it on Friday; a Jewish youth group from West Berlin is coming over and a TV camera team from Israel will be there too. It'll be something you really should see.'

I did go on the Friday evening. By the time I had crossed the border at Friedrichstrasse, it was too late to take the bus, so I arrived in an unlicensed taxi. The driver, who approached me at the taxi stand, was wearing Western jeans, a leather jacket, and a Lech Walesa mustache. The car and everything in it were Japanese. When I told him I wanted to go to the synagogue, his face became animated: 'Really? Some of my friends told me that they've fixed up the synagogue and they now have a Rabbi. I've never been in a synagogue; do you think anyone would mind if I come?' I didn't think anyone would mind: so he and I walked in together.

There were a hundred people in the synagogue, of whom about thirty were members of the West Berlin Jewish Youth Group. There was no Israeli camera crew – I was told they were on strike. The congregation had just finished the Friday evening service, and the Rabbi called the West Berliners to bring the Torahs out of the Ark: as he did, the Cantor, with a disapproving look, stepped down from the platform, and joined the congregation. But before the Torah procession, Rabbi Neumann interrupted the service, and made an announcement. 'I can't always bring you good news, but today I can. This afternoon I heard that Matthias Rust (the West German sports pilot) is going home, and Ida Nudel got her exit visa to Israel.' No reaction. Did they not understand?

Rabbi Neumann and the West German adolescents – bouncy in their sweatshirts, blue jeans, and Addidas – paraded the Torahs up and down the aisle of the synagogue; they sang, and they danced. The kids seemed disoriented in this strange environment, and they took their cues exclusively from the Rabbi. The East Berliners watched politely, but did not join in. When the Torahs had been replaced and the *Kiddush* (the blessing over wine) chanted, Rabbi Neumann invited the gathering to a reception for the West Berliners in the *Sukkah*, a small wooden hut decorated and covered with branches of trees and fruits and vegetables from the harvest.

Carefully decorated with apples, red peppers, and horse-chestnuts, the *Sukkah* on the Rykestrasse proved beautiful and cozy, but too small to contain more than the West Berlin youths and a dozen or so East Berliners: the rest poked their heads in briefly and went home. A light dinner of eggs, salads, cheese, soft drinks, and chalah was provided by one of the members of the East Berlin Jewish Community: the eating was punctuated by the self-consciously hearty singing of Rabbi Neumann and the West Berlin youth group – *Hevenu Shalom Aleichem*, (We Bring Peace to You) *Am Yisrael Chai*, (The People of Israel lives) *David Melech Yisrael*, (David, King of Israel) *Zion Zion Zion* – loud singing, loud clapping in a small and crowded *Sukkah*. In the middle, Rabbi Neumann performed a solo in Russian – 'Moses said unto Pharaoh, Let my people go.' The East Berliners listened to all this quietly. The Rabbi ended the evening by reminding those gathered that, although Germany is a land of cemeteries, Simchat Torah is a celebration of life, and Jews also have to learn to live. He thanked the West Berliners for bringing so much life to East Berlin and, on a more somber note, he quoted Rabbi Nachman of Brazlav: 'Life is a narrow bridge, and the most important thing is not to be afraid.'

I left the *Sukkah* with two friends from East Berlin, Boris and David, both men in their thirties who grew up in secular families in the Communist Party, but who have recently become interested in getting back in touch with their Jewishness. David was starting the new year by wearing a real *kipah* to synagogue for the first time: white with gold embroidery, it had been sent him by a close friend now living in the West. Until it arrived, David had been attending services in a beret inherited from his father who had been wounded in the Spanish Civil War. At first it seemed like we might spend the evening with some of the kids from West Berlin who were heading for the Alexanderplatz, but then David decided not to: 'There are too many of them, they're too noisy, and they make me nervous. I think I'd rather spend the evening with you. Have you ever been to the restaurant at the Palast Hotel?'

Two other young East Berlin Jews joined us, and we passed the rest of the evening at the Palast, where any potential *joie de vivre* or Sabbath merriment was immediately suffocated by the stiff waiters and the overly-heavy chandeliers. A very personal and difficult discussion developed around what had been, for the East Berlin Jewish Community, a month of unusually intense activity and many new experiences. As I had no permission to conduct interviews that night, I am using pseudonyms and changing some facts in the interest of relating the feelings of some of East Berlin's younger Jews during those weeks. David began:

'You know, Robin, for decades all we had here of Jewish life was prayer services on the Sabbath and holidays and one cultural event a month from October through May. Now, all of a sudden, we also have a new Rabbi, Hebrew classes every Tuesday, meetings of our group of younger Jews every second or third Monday, and a children's programme on Sunday mornings. Sometimes it just seems to be too much too fast. I'm not used to it.'

'Is that why there weren't many children there tonight?'

'No. Some of us celebrated *Simchat Torah* last night.'

'But the Rabbi told me you were celebrating it tonight. That's why I came.'

'Well, the Rabbi decided to celebrate tonight, but the Board of Directors has never moved a Jewish holiday before, and they held a celebration last night: that was when *we* danced and sang and brought candy for our children. Rabbi Neumann doesn't care how we feel: he's here for the West Germans and the Israeli television.'

'Why didn't you want to have coffee with the kids from West Berlin tonight?'

'There were too many of them: there was no way to break into that group and make contact. Besides which, that kind of loud singing and cheering reminds me of the Hitler Youth. Here, being Jewish means assuming a quieter, more reflective attitude, and I feel more comfortable with that.'

Boris is a writer who, at synagogue, covers his tangled blond hair with a dark blue *kipah* his grandfather brought out of Germany in 1933 and back into Germany in 1949. He was also offended by the visitors from West Berlin:

'Those young West German Jews coming here and making a big show of self-confidence and strength is basically a lie. I've attended professional conferences in West Berlin and Munich, and I've seen how the Jews live there: they have police stationed outside the synagogues and the Jewish schools. We have other problems, but it would never occur to anyone here that Jews or synagogues need police protection. I've also read interviews with West German Jews where they've articulated their anxieties and the anti-Semitism they put up with daily. Why do they send their adolescents here to pretend everything's wonderful there? No politician here could build a career on remarks about Jews and cash registers.'

I tried to answer:

'Everything you say may be true, but I think the Jews who are fearful are those born during and before the 1950s. West German Jews born after 1960 seem to feel much more comfortable in their surroundings.'

'That may mean their parents are trying to protect them and give them a false sense of security; but even with that, everything you have to know about the situation of Jews in West Germany is right in the newspapers. By the way, some of those kids were speaking Hebrew with the Rabbi. Were they from Israel?·'

'No. They were speaking Hebrew with a German accent.'

'So, if they're German, why were they talking Hebrew?'

David objected to the Zionist content of many of the songs:

'I don't always agree with our government, and I don't think we're being told all there is to know about Israel. I know there's a peace movement there, though it's never mentioned in our press. But still, I don't think we're a chosen people, and I'm not a Zionist. I have no interest in learning most of the songs they were screaming in my ear.'

Sarah had until then been silent. Born in Amsterdam in 1946, the daughter of a Party functionary, she is now an editor with an East Berlin publishing house. She was particularly bitter:

'In a way, the Rabbi is playing right into the hands of the Party. They want an opening to the West, they know about the Jewish lobby in Washington, and they know that German–Jewish feature stories sell to the media. In bringing those kids over here, Rabbi Neumann is giving the government all the good publicity it wants.'

Boris resolved the tension:

'Judaism derives its greatness from the fact that it's a world religion, influenced by many cultures and traditions. When the Jewish Community here became isolated in the 1950s, we became provincial,

and our Judaism too became impoverished. Now there is again openness
and new ideas, but the price of our thirty years of isolation is that the
news from abroad is coming from an American Rabbi with some
Reaganite tendencies. My Jewishness has never been more than one
part of my identity. I'm also half German, half Russian, a writer, and
a third-generation Communist. But there are a lot of things I like
about this Rabbi, and I'm going to come around to some of the events
at the Jewish Community to see what develops from all this.'

There is definitely movement in East Berlin's Jewish Community,
though its scope and ultimate direction remain unclear. Because the
German Democratic Republic is neither a Western-style democracy nor
a multi-ethnic society, its Jewish Community will not assume an active
role in ethnic politics and community development as it does in the USA
and Canada. A Soviet scenario is equally unlikely: most of East Berlin's
young Jews are not dissidents and they don't want to live in Israel. The
Jewish Community will probably play an important role in the slowly
developing ties between the German Democratic Republic and Israel.
And the definition of the Jewish Community as a religious organization
may have to be officially or *de facto* altered if it is to accommodate a
considerable number of atheists. One of the many challenges to the
Honecker government and the Jewish Community in the coming months
and years, then, will be the redefinition and reintegration of the Jewish
Community in a way that will prove constructive for the society at large,
and for its Jewish population.

Notes

CHAPTER 1: INTRODUCTION

1. All population statistics in this paragraph are found in H.G. Sellenthin (1959) p. 101.
2. Berlin Museum, *Synagogen in Berlin*, Vol. I (1982) p. 5.
3. *Encyclopaedia Judaica* (1972), Vol. 4, p. 652.
4. AJDC Report on Berlin, 21 February 1946, New York #282, stencilled, p. 3.
5. Julius Meyer, an Auschwitz survivor, was active among the leadership of the Berlin Jewish Community. In the early 1950s he was a Deputy in the East German *Volkskammer* (Parliament) and Chairman of the Association of Jewish Communities of the German Democratic Republic. In early January 1953 he fled to West Berlin. See interview with Peter Kirchner, p. 15.
6. AJDC Report on Berlin, 21 February 1946, New York #282, stencilled; and Berlin Report, 31 May 1946, New York #355, stencilled.
7. Thompson (1967) p. 14. The following pages draw heavily on Thompson's extremely thorough reconstruction of the anti-Jewish measures in the GDR in the early 1950s.
8. Rabbi Nathan Peter Levinson was born in Berlin in 1921. He emigrated to the USA in 1941 where he became a Rabbi in 1948. From 1950 to 1953 he served as Rabbi in Berlin.
9. Martin Riesenburger (1896–1965) never became an ordained Rabbi. He studied at the *Hochschule für Wissenschaft des Judentums* (The Centre for the Scientific Study of Judaism and Rabbinical Seminary), and served the Berlin Jewish Community throughout the Nazi period as a lay preacher, first for the Jewish Home for the Aged, and then at the Weissensee Cemetery. The Nazis allowed him to remain in Berlin throughout the twelve years of the Third Reich because they needed someone to bury the Jewish dead, and because he was then living in a 'privileged mixed marriage'. His wife converted to Judaism after the war. For further information see Alan Abrams (1985) pp. 97–102.

CHAPTER 3: SONJA BERNE

1. Oberkantor Estrongo Nachama has served for many years as Cantor for the synagogue on the Pestalozzistrasse in West Berlin, though he also sings regularly for the Jewish Community in East Berlin and for the American congregation in Berlin.
2. Öljean Ingster, a retired economist, currently serves as Cantor for the Jewish Community in East Berlin.
3. The *Tribüne* is the journal of the FDGB (Confederation of Free German Trade Unions) in the GDR.

CHAPTER 4: DR HERMANN SIMON

1. Rabbi Ernst Stein, the spiritual leader of the (Liberal) synagogue on the Pestalozzistrasse in West Berlin, frequently officiates at weddings, funerals, etc. and serves as an advisor to the East Berlin Jewish Community.
2. In the first third of this century the synagogue on the Oranienburgerstrasse was one of Berlin's largest, most elegant, and religiously most dynamic Liberal congregations.

CHAPTER 5: DR IRENE RUNGE

1. 'Susannah', in Joachim Walther (ed.) *Brennesselsuppe und Hiatiti: Erzählte Kindheit* (Buchverlag Der Morgen, (East) Berlin, 1983) pp. 341–9.
2. The Nuremberg Laws of 15 September 1935 denied German citizenship to Jews and, among other measures, forbade marriage and sexual relations between Jews and German citizens. Regulations for the implementation of these laws referred to paternity as the criterion for determining Jewishness, although, according to Jewish law, Jewishness is acquired from the mother.
3. Rolf Bothe (ed.) *Synagogen in Berlin*, 2 vols (Verlag Willmuth Arenhövel, (West) Berlin, 1983).
4. Eike Geisel, *Im Scheunenviertel* (Severin und Siedler, (West) Berlin, 1981). The *Scheunenviertel*, a neighbourhood in what is now East Berlin, was, in the first third of this century, densely inhabited by poor Jews who had recently immigrated to Berlin from Eastern Europe.
5. The Herbert Baum Group in Berlin was the only Jewish resistance group operating within Nazi Germany. In 1942 they were exposed by an informer and all but two members of the group were executed (see interview with Thomas Eckert).

CHAPTER 7: JALDA REBLING

1. The Wall separating the two Berlins was built in 1961. Thus the implication is that those who painted the swastikas may have come over from the West.
2. Eugen Gollomb was the President of the Jewish Community in Leipzig. He died in January 1988.
3. The film *Holocaust* was produced in the USA and broadcast over the West German television network which is received in most parts of the GDR.
4. *Sovietish Heimland* is a Jewish periodical published in the Soviet Union.
5. Ilmenau is a city in the south-western part of the GDR.

CHAPTER 8: DR VINCENT VON WROBLEWSKY

1. Before the Fascist period Ullstein Verlag was an important Jewish-owned publishing house in Berlin. After the Second World War it became integrated into the Springer enterprises which include, besides Ullstein books, several major West German newspapers and magazines.
2. This committee was formed to fight for the liberation of Dimitroff, a leader

of the Bulgarian Communist Party who was accused of setting fire to the German Parliament.
3. This is a reference to the fact that as of 1 January 1939, all Jewish females in Germany were required to assume the first name Sara.
4. An Orthodox Jewish Community would not recognize Sarah as a Jew because she has a non-Jewish mother.
5. Heinz Knobloch, *Herr Moses in Berlin* (Buchverlag Der Morgen, (East) Berlin, 1979).

CHAPTER 9: CLARA BERLINER

1. The synagogue on the Fasanenstrasse, one of prewar Berlin's largest and most elegant Jewish houses of worship, was attended largely by the Liberal upper-middle-class Jews of Charlottenburg.
2. Anna Seghers, Stefan Hermlin, and Peter Edel are considered among the most important Jewish writers in the German Democratic Republic.
3. The National Front is the umbrella organization consisting of all the political parties in the GDR.
4. Oberkantor Estrongo Nachama has served for many years as Cantor for the synagogue on the Pestalozzistrasse in West Berlin, though he also sings regularly for the *Jüdische Gemeinde* in East Berlin and for the American congregation in Berlin.
5. Hans Leberecht is the GDR press and radio correspondent in Tel Aviv.

CHAPTER 10: DR ALFRED KATZENSTEIN

1. *L'Humanité* is the daily journal of the French Communist Party. During the Nazi occupation it was published illegally.
2. Harry Kemelman, *Friday the Rabbi Slept Late* (Crown Publishers, New York, 1964).

CHAPTER 13: HELMUT ESCHWEGE

1. See Konrad Kwiet, 'Historians of the German Democratic Republic on Anti-semitism and Persecution', in *Leo Baeck Institute Year Book*, Vol. XXI (1976) pp. 173–98.
2. Gustave Stresemann (1878–1929) was Chancellor of the German Reich for a short time in 1923 and Foreign Minister from 1923 to 1929. Although a nationalist and a conservative, Stresemann pursued a policy of re-establishing normal relations with the Western powers after the First World War.
3. The Palestine Communist Party affiliated with the Comintern in 1924. Throughout the 1920s and 1930s its history was characterized by internal fragmentation – including alternating cooperation and friction between Jewish and Arab members – and conflicts with the Zionists and the British.
4. Laszlo Rajk was a veteran of the Spanish Civil War, and a prominent Communist and Minister of the Interior in Hungary in the early post-war years. He was executed in 1949 after a show trial in which he was demonstrated to be a national deviationist and an imperialist agent.

5. Usually only GDR citizens who have reached the age of retirement are allowed to travel to the West.

CHAPTER 14: AFTERWORD

1. See 'Deutsche, Linke, Juden', *Äesthetik und Kommunikation*, No. 51, June 1983.
2. 'A most delicate situation arose recently when both eastern and western Authorities made an attempt to mobilize the *Gemeinde's* public opinion. Western authorities demanded a resolution in protest against the anti-Semitic trial of Slansky and the other Jewish convicts in Prague, while at the same time a request came forward from the official eastern quarters that the *Gemeinde* should pass a resolution and dispatch a telegram to Washington in protest against the 'anti-Semitic' trial and conviction of Julius and Ethel Rosenberg...the outcome... was that both requests have been declined.' AJDC Paris Letter No., 130, *Newsletter on Jewish Life in Berlin*, 6 March 1953.
3. *European Jewry Ten Years After the War* (Institute of Jewish Affairs of the World Jewish Congress, New York, 1956) p. 147.
4. At least one of the interviewees in this volume has a relative who worked indirectly for the military of a major Western country.
5. Personal communication, Eugene Du Bow, winter 1986.
6. Personal conversation, 20 April 1986, New York.
7. See Everett C. Hughes (1948/1962). Interestingly enough, this essay was inspired by Hughes' observations during his visit to West Germany in 1948.
8. In fall 1985, the Christian Democratic mayor of the small West German town of Korschenbroich was removed from office after suggesting publicly that killing a few rich Jews would help balance the budget.
9. Also in fall 1985, a scandal arose when a theatre in Frankfurt attempted to stage a play by Fassbinder, *Garbage, the City, and Death*, which utilized the concept of the Jew as a rich and ruthless real estate speculator, responsible for inner-city decay in West Germany. At the play's premiere, members of the Jewish Community mounted the stage and prevented the performance.

Bibliography

Abrams, Alan (1985) *Special Treatment: The Untold Story of Hitler's Third Race* (Secaucus: Lyle Stuart Inc.).

Agee, Joel (1975) *Twelve Years: An American Boyhood in East Germany* (New York: Farrar, Straus Giroux).

Ahren, Yizhak, (1984) 'Vom Aussterben bedroht: Die Lage der jüdischen Gemeinden in der DDR', *Tribüne*, no. 92, pp. 78–85.

Allgemeiner Studentenauschuss der Technischen Universität Berlin (1984) *Die Berliner Widerstandsgruppe um Herbert Baum* (Berlin: ASTA-Druckerei).

American Jewish Committee (1949) *Proceedings of the Heidelberg Conference on the Future of Jewish Communities in Germany* (New York).

Arendt, Hannah (1958) *The Origins of Totalitarianism* (Cleveland and New York: The World Publishing Company).

Bahro, Rudolf (1978) *The Alternative in Eastern Europe* (London: Verso).

Bahro, Rudolf (1984) *From Red to Green: Interviews with New Left Review* (London: Verso).

Baker, Leonard (1978) *Days of Sorrow and Pain: Leo Baeck and the Berlin Jews* (New York: Macmillan).

Balfour, Michael (1982) *West Germany: A Contemporary History* (London & Canberra: Croom Helm).

Bary, Hermann (ed.) (1954) *European Jewish Year Book: Jewish Life in Europe* (Frankfurt: Union).

Berlin Museum (1983) *Synagogen in Berlin*, 2 vols ((West) Berlin: Verlag Willmuth Arenhövel).

B'nai B'rith (1960) *Mission to Germany: The report of a mission to Germany during the summer of 1960 by ten B'nai B'rith representatives* (New York: stencilled).

Bodemann, Y. Michal (1983) 'Opfer zu Komplizen gemacht? Der jüdisch-deutsch Bruch und die verlorene Identität: Anmerkungen zu einer Rückkehr in die Bundesrepublik', *Die Zeit*, No. 1–30, December, p. 28.

Bodemann, Y. Michal (1985) 'Die "Überwölbung" von Auschwitz. Der jüdische Faktor in der Mythology der Wende-Republik', *Ästhetik und Kommunikation*, vol. 15, no. 56, pp. 43–8.

Bodemann, Y. Michal (1986) 'Staat und Ethnizität: Der Aufbau der Jüdischer Gemeinden im Kalten Krieg', in Michal Brumlik *et al.* (eds) *Jüdisches Leben in Deutschland seit 1945* (Frankfurt: Athenäum Verlag).

Broder, Henryk M. and Lang, Michel (eds) *Fremd im eigenen Land: Juden in der Bundesrepublik* (Frankfurt: Fischer Taschenbuch Verlag).

(1983) *Christians and Churches. A Report from the German Democratic Republic*, 2nd edn ((East) Berlin: Panorama).

(1983) 'Deutsche, Linke, Juden', *Ästhetik und Kommunikation*, no. 51, (Berlin)

Elcott, David Marvin (1981) 'The Political Resocialization of German Jews in Palestine 1933–39', unpublished PhD Thesis, Columbia University, New York.

Elsner, Eckert (1974) 'Juden in Berlin', in *Emuna*, pp. 3–16.

(1972) *Encyclopaedia Judaica* (Jerusalem: Keter Publishing House).

Eschwege, Helmut (1970) 'Resistance of German Jews against the Nazi Regime', in *Leo Baeck Institute Year Book*, Vol. XV (London) pp. 143–80.

Etzold, Alfred, Kirchner, Dr Peter and Knobloch, Heinz (1979) *Jüdische Friedhöfe in Berlin* ((East) Berlin: Institut für Denkmalpflege).

Galliner, Nickie (1972–73) 'The Jewish Community of East-Berlin', in *Schalom Dialoge*, nos. 22–23, pp. 41–4.

Gaus, Günter (1983) *Wo Deutschland liegt: Eine Ortsbestimmung* (Hamburg: Hoffman und Campe).

Girardet, Cella (1984) 'Juden in der DDR: eine aussterbende Minderheit?' in *Neue Züricher Zeitung*, 22 September, p. 42.

Harman, Chris (1983) *Class Struggles in Eastern Europe: 1945–83*, 2nd edn (London and Sydney: Pluto Press).

Heilbut, Anthony (1983) *Exiled in Paradise: German Refugee Artists and Intellectuals in America, From the 1930s to the Present* (Boston: Beacon Press).

Henry, Frances (1984) *Victims and Neighbors: A Small Town in Nazi Germany Remembered* (South Hadley: Bergin & Garvey).

Hermann, Klaus J. (1982) 'Political and Social Dimensions of the Jewish Communities in the GDR', *Nationalities Papers*, vol. X, no. 1, Spring, pp. 41–54.

Hermlin, Stephan (1983) *Äusserungen 1944–1982* ((East) Berlin and Weimar: Aufbau Verlag).

Heym, Stefan (1973) *The King David Report* (London: Hodder and Stoughton).

Heym, Stefan (1984) *The Wandering Jew* (New York: Holt, Rinehart & Winston).

Hirt-Manheimer, Aron (1981) 'Ten Days in East Germany: Communists of Jewish Descent', *Reform Judaism*, February 9.

Holm, Hans Axel (1970) *The Other Germans: Report from an East German Town* (New York: Pantheon Books).

Hughes, Everett C. (1962) 'Good People and Dirty Work', in *The Sociological Eye* (Chicago and New York: Aldine Atherton) pp. 87–97.

Jouhy, Ernest (1960) 'German Youth & German History', in *Commentary*, April, pp. 308–14.

Katcher, Leo (1968) *Post Mortem: The Jews and Germany Now* (London: Hamish Hamilton).

Kirchner, Peter (1974) 'Die Jüdische Gemeinde in der Hauptstadt der Deutschen Demokratischen Republik', in *Emuna*, March–April, pp. 111–14.

Knobloch, Heinz (1984) *Herr Moses in Berlin: Ein Menschenfreund in Preussen; Das Leben des Moses Mendelssohn* (Berlin: Das Arsenal).

Kwiet, Konrad (1976) 'Historians of the German Democratic Republic on Antisemitism and Persecution', in *Leo Baeck Institute Year Book*, vol. XXI (London) pp. 173–98.

Kwiet, Konrad and Helmut Eschwege (1984) *Selbstbehauptung und Widerstand: Deutsche Juden im Kampf um Existenz und Menschenwurde 1933–1945* (Hamburg: Hans Christians Verlag).

Lehrman, Hal (1953) 'The New Germany and Her Remaining Jews', *Commentary*, December, pp. 513–24.

Lesser, Andrew (1973) 'Jews and the DDR', unpublished manuscript, Lanchester Polytechnic, Coventry, England.

Levine, Herbert S. (1975) 'Munich Thirty Years Later: Trying to Erase the Shadow', in *Present Tense*, Spring, pp. 31–5.

Levkov, Ilya (1980) 'Russian Jews in West Berlin', in *Midstream*, June–July, pp. 19–25.

Lewis, Stephen (1984) *Art out of Agony: The Holocaust Theme in Literature, Sculpture, and Film* (Toronto: CBC Enterprises) Chapter 5, Jurek Becker.

Lichtheim, George (1957) 'A Berlin Notebook: Parochial Capital', in *Commentary*, pp. 292–301.

Lust, Peter (1966) *Two Germanies: Mirror of an Age* (Montreal: Harvest House).

Madrasch-Groschop, Ursula (1983) *Die Weltbühne: Porträt einer Zeitschrift* ((East) Berlin: Buchverlag Der Morgen).

Maor, Harry (1961) 'Über den Wiederaufbau der jüdischen Gemeinden in Deutschland seit 1945', unpublished dissertation, Mainz University.

Markovits, Andrei S. (1984) 'Germans and Jews: The Continuation of an Uneasy Relationship', in *Jewish Frontier*, vol. LI, no. 4. April.

Marx, Karl (1963) *Early Writings*, translated and edited by T.B. Bottomore (New York: McGraw-Hill)

Mühlen, Norbert (1962) *The Survivors: A Report on the Jews in Germany Today* (New York: Thomas Y. Crowell)

(1961–) *Nachrichtenblatt des Verbandes der Jüdischen Gemeinden in der DDR*.

Newmann, Franz (1944) *Behemoth: The Structure and Practice of National Socialism 1933–1944* (New York: Oxford University Press).

(1974–1984) *New German Critique*, Milwaukee: University of Wisconsin-Milwaukee, Nos 2, 3, 19–21, 31.

Nolte, Ernst (1966) *Three Faces of Fascism: Action Française, Italian Fascism, National Socialism* (New York: Holt, Rinehart & Winston).

Richarz, Monika (1985) 'Jews in Today's Germanies', in *Leo Baeck Institute Year Book*, vol. XXX (London) pp. 126–30.

Risenburger, Martin (1960) *Das Licht Verlöschte nicht*. ((East)Berlin: Union Verlag).

Robinson, Nechemiah (1954) *Survey of Events in Jewish Life, 1953* (New York: Institute of Jewish Affairs, World Jewish Congress) pp. 81–7.

Schultz, Hans Jürgen (ed). (1978) *Mein Judentum* (Stuttgart, Berlin; Kreuz Verlag).

Sellenthin, H.G. (1959) *Geschichte der Juden in Berlin und des Gebäudes Fasanenstrasse 79–80: Festschrift anlässlich der Einweihung des Jüdischen Gemeindehauses* (Berlin).

Shirer, William L. (1959) *The Rise and Fall of the Third Reich: A History of Nazi Germany* (New York: Simon & Schuster).

Sichrovsky, Peter (1985) *Wir wissen nicht was Morgen wird, wir wissen wohl was gestern war: Junge Juden in Deutschland und Österreich* (Köln: Kiepenheuer & Witsch).

Simon, Hermann (1983) *Das Berliner Jüdische Museum in der Oranienburger Strasse: Geschichte einer zerstorten Kulturstätte* (Berlin: Berlin Museum).

Strauss, H.A. (1970) *Gegenwart im Rückblick: Festgabe für die Jüdische Gemeinde zu Berlin, 25 Jahre nach dem Neubeginn* (Heidelberg: Lothar Stiehm Verlag).

Thompson, Gerald Eugene (1967) 'The Political Status of the Jews in the German Democratic Republic since 1945', unpublished MA thesis, University of Iowa.

Walther, Joachim (ed.) (1983) *Brennesselsuppe und Hiatiti: Erzählte Kindheit* ((East) Berlin: Buchverlag Der Morgen).

(1946–48) *Der Weg* (Berlin).

von Wroblewsky, Vincent (1983) 'Karl Jaspers' Innere Emigration: Schuld und Sühne eines einsamen Deutschen', in *Dialektik 7: Antifascismus oder Niederlagen beweisen nichts, als dass wir wenige sind* (Köln: Pahl-Rugenstein Verlag).

Weltsch, Robert (1946) 'Berliner Tagebuch', in *Yedioth, Jerusalem*, 3 February, pp. 5–6.

Wetzel, Heinz (ed.) (1983) 'Moral Issues in Jurek Becker's *Jacob der Lügner*: Contributions to a Symposium', in *Seminar: A Journal of Germanic Studies*, Fall, pp. 265–92.
Wolf, Christa (1980) *Patterns of Childhood* (New York: Farrar, Straus & Giroux).

Glossary

Bund Deutscher Mädel (BDM): the female youth organization of the Nazi Party in Germany.

Central-Verein Deutscher Staatsburger Jüdischen Glaubens (CV, Central Union of German Citizens of the Jewish Faith): this organization was founded in Berlin in 1893 to defend Jewish civil and social equality against increasing German anti-Semitism. The CV rejected both Zionism and internationalism.

Cohanim: descendants of the priestly tribe of Cohen, Cohanim have special ritual functions.

Cultural Sundays: the *Jüdische Gemeinde* organizes a Jewish cultural event one Sunday a month from October through May.

Deutsche Demokratische Republik (DDR, East Germany, GDR): these terms are all used interchangeably to refer to the German Democratic Republic.

Deutsche Volkspartei (German People's Party): a nationalist liberal party formed in 1918, and headed by Gustav Stresemann (see Chapter 13 note 2). After Stresemann's death, the party moved toward the right, and in 1933 it merged with the National Socialists.

Ernst Thälmann Junge Pionere (Pioneers): the childrens' extension of the FDJ (see below).

Freie Deutsche Jugend (FDJ, Free German Youth): the youth movement in the GDR.

Gauleiter: a high functionary in charge of the entire National Socialist Party apparatus of one of the 43 *Gaue*, or regions, into which Nazi Germany was divided.

Geltungsjude: the term used by the Nazis to designate persons of mixed parentage professing the Jewish religion.

Hitler Jugend (HJ, Hitler Youth): the male youth organization of the Nazi Party in Germany.

Jüdische Gemeinde (*Gemeinde*, Jewish Community): these terms are used interchangeably to refer to East Berlin's official and only Jewish organization.

Jungdeutsche Orden (Young German Order): an anti-Bolshevik organization founded in 1918 by veterans of the First World War.

163

Kristallnacht (Night of Broken Glass, 9 November 1938): the first official pogrom of the Nazi regime.

Mikveh: a Jewish ritual bath.

Minyan: a quorum of, traditionally, ten men required for the carrying out of a complete prayer service.

Mohel: a functionary of the Jewish community who performs ritual circumcisions.

Organization Todt (OT, Todt Organization): named after its founder Fritz Todt (1891–1942), this organization was responsible for most of the physical infrastructure of the Third Reich including the Western Wall and the extension of the German highway system into the occupied territories.

Reichstagsbrand (burning down of the German Parliament building on 27 February 1933): 'The *Reichstag* fire, blamed on the Communist Party in defiance of all reason and probability, provided, with the ensuing emergency regulations of the decree "For Protection of People and State", the legal basis for twelve years of National Socialist rule.' Ernst Nolte, *Three Faces of Fascism* (Holt, Rinehart and Winston, New York, 1966) p. 345.

Reichsvereinigung der Juden in Deutschland (Alliance of Jews in Germany): an organization imposed on the Jews in Germany by the Nazis in 1939 to replace the Jews' own umbrella organization, the *Reichsvertretung der Deutschen Juden* (Representation of German Jews). The *Reichsvereinigung* was charged with the administration of Jewish affairs under the Nazi government. The extent of the *Reichsvereinigung's* autonomy and/or collaboration with the Nazis is the subject of considerable debate. See Baker (1978) Chapter 11.

Slansky Trial: the first of a series of anti-Semitic show trials held in Czechoslovakia in the early 1950s. Rudolf Slansky (1901–52), then Secretary General of the Czechoslovak Communist Party, was the most prominent of fourteen Party members prosecuted for conspiracy against the state. Eleven of the fourteen accused were Jewish. Slansky was executed in 1952.

Sozialistische Arbeiterpartei (SAP, Socialist German Workers Party): one of the many small groupings of the Left in Palestine in the 1930s and 40s.

Sozialistische Einheitspartei Deutschland (SED, Socialist Unity Party, 'the Party'): the German Democratic Republic has more than one political party, but this party dominates the political life of the nation.

Stahlhelm (Nationalist Association of Former Servicemen): a monarchist group organized in 1918 to oppose the German revolution. In 1933 Hitler, fearing potential opposition, incorporated the *Stahlhelm* into the SA (see below).

Sturmabteilung (SA, Storm Troups, Brown Shirts): one of the élite groups within Hitler's armed forces. In 1933 they were responsible for staging Hitler's massive parades and rallies, and for supervising the boycott of Jewish businesses and professionals. They were later dissolved, and their role was taken over by the SS.

Vereinigung der Verfolgten des Nazi Regimes (Alliance of Persecutees of the Nazi Regime, VVN): an organization founded in 1947 in Berlin to protect the rights of Jews and non-Jews persecuted by the Nazis. In the early post-war years it had a clientele of 50 000 in Berlin. All parties were represented in the VVN, though Jews and Communists were particularly prominent among the leadership, and most Jews in the GDR were members.

Verfolgte des Naziregimes (Persecutees of the Nazi Regime, VDN): currently the official institution in the GDR responsible for the recognition and care of those politically and racially persecuted by the Nazis.

Youth Group: the *Jüdische Gemeinde*'s programme for its younger members and prospective members.

Index

DATE		